A Father

GOD
BLESSES

BY

JACK COUNTRYMAN

A Division of Thomas Nelson Publishers

THOMAS NELSON
Since 1798

NASHVILLE   MEXICO CITY   RIO DE JANEIRO

Published in Nashville, Tennessee, by Thomas Nelson. Thomas Nelson is a registered trademark of HarperCollins Christian Publishing, Inc.

Thomas Nelson titles may be purchased in bulk for educational, business, fund-raising, or sales promotional use. For information, please e-mail SpecialMarkets@ ThomasNelson.com.

Scripture quotations are taken from the NEW KING JAMES VERSION®. © 1982 by Thomas Nelson. Used by permission. All rights reserved.

ISBN-13: 978-1-4003-2430-9

Printed in China

15 16 17 18 19 TIMS 5 4 3 2 1

www.thomasnelson.com

CONTENTS

Introduction vii

GOD BLESSES YOU WHEN YOU . . .

Instruct Your Children in His Word 2

Teach Your Children to Pray 8

Show Kindness to Your Family 13

Teach Your Children Gratitude 16

Reach Out to Families Who Are Homeless 20

Love Your Neighbors 25

Comfort Your Children in Their Sorrow 29

Ask for His Patience 32

Seek His Spirit's Guidance 36

Admit Your Shortcomings as a Father 41

Have the Courage to Be a Man of Integrity 47

GOD LISTENS TO YOUR PRAYERS WHEN . . .

You Seek His Wisdom for Your Children 54

You Are Overwhelmed with Your Family
    Responsibilities 58

You Seek His Forgiveness When You Wrong
    Your Family 63

You Feel Depressed and Lose Your Way 66

Your Children Disappoint You 69
You Trust Him Even When You Don't Understand 73
You Trust Him When You Wait for His Answers 75
You Claim Victory Over the Sins in Your Life 79
You Dedicate Your Life to Christ 84

GOD'S SPECIAL LOVE IS WITH YOU WHEN . . .

You Bring Problems to Him 90
You Rely on Him to Guide and Direct Your
    Children 95
You Forgive Your Children When They've
    Done Wrong 99
You Bring Your Family Together to Pray 103
You Share Your Family's Blessings with the Poor 106
You Dedicate Your Children to the Lord 109

GOD ENCOURAGES YOU TO . . .

Teach Your Children the Love of God 114
Grow in Your Own Christian Walk 119
Share Your Faith with Your Children. 123
Deal Honestly with Those Close to You 128
Never Stop Loving Your Wife 132
Be Wise with Your Family Finances 137
Bring Your Tithe to the Storehouse 142

GOD COMFORTS YOU WHEN . . .

You Feel Inadequate in Raising Your Children. 148
Your Child Is Seriously Ill 153
Your Wife Doesn't Seem to Understand 157
You Must Discipline Your Children 161
You Feel Powerless to Shield Your Children 164

GOD FILLS YOU WITH JOY WHEN . . .

Your Family Worships Together. 170
Your Children Grow to Love Him. 173
Your Family Gives Praises to the Lord. 177
Your Children Who Know His Love, Share It
    with Others 181

GOD HONORS YOU WHEN YOU . . .

Make a Stand Against Worldliness 186
Set Aside Your Pride 190
Choose to Speak Carefully 193
Give to God's Work 195
Develop a Discerning Spirit 198

INTRODUCTION

God desires to bless every father with wisdom from His Word. As a father, you have been given the responsibility of raising and guiding the development of children in today's world. *A Father God Blesses* is filled with forty-seven topics that have been created to offer help and encouragement for various situations in life. May you rely and trust in the loving relationship the Father has for you as you read these topical passages from God's Word.

GOD BLESSES YOU WHEN YOU . . .

Instruct Your Children in His Word

Hear, my children, the instruction of a father,
    And give attention to know understanding;
    For I give you good doctrine:
    Do not forsake my law.
    When I was my father's son,
    Tender and the only one in the sight of my
        mother,
    He also taught me, and said to me:
    "Let your heart retain my words;
    Keep my commands, and live."

Proverbs 4:1–4

All Scripture is given by inspiration of God, and is profitable for doctrine, for reproof, for correction, for instruction in righteousness.

2 Timothy 3:16

For the word of God is living and powerful, and sharper than any two-edged sword, piercing even to the division of soul and spirit, and of joints and marrow, and is a discerner of the thoughts and intents of the heart.

HEBREWS 4:12

A wise man will hear and increase learning,
And a man of understanding will attain
    wise counsel,
To understand a proverb and an enigma,
The words of the wise and their riddles.
The fear of the LORD is the beginning of
    knowledge,
But fools despise wisdom and instruction.
My son, hear the instruction of your father,
And do not forsake the law of your mother;
For they will be a graceful ornament on
    your head,
And chains about your neck.

PROVERBS 1:5–9

Give ear, O my people, to my law;
    Incline your ears to the words of my mouth.
    I will open my mouth in a parable;
    I will utter dark sayings of old,
    Which we have heard and known,
    And our fathers have told us.
    We will not hide them from their children,
    Telling to the generation to come the praises of
        the LORD,
    And His strength and His wonderful works that
        He has done.
    For He established a testimony in Jacob,
    And appointed a law in Israel,
    Which He commanded our fathers,
    That they should make them known to their
        children;
    That the generation to come might know them,
    The children who would be born,
    That they may arise and declare them to their
        children,
    That they may set their hope in God,
    And not forget the works of God,

But keep His commandments;
And may not be like their fathers,
A stubborn and rebellious generation,
A generation that did not set its heart aright,
And whose spirit was not faithful to God.

PSALM 78:1–8

My son, give attention to my words;
Incline your ear to my sayings.
Do not let them depart from your eyes;
Keep them in the midst of your heart;
For they are life to those who find them,
And health to all their flesh.

PROVERBS 4:20–22

"All flesh is as grass,
And all the glory of man as the flower of the
grass.
The grass withers,
And its flower falls away,
But the word of the LORD endures forever."

1 PETER 1:24–25

"Now therefore, listen to me, my children,
    For blessed are those who keep my ways.
    Hear instruction and be wise,
    And do not disdain it.
    Blessed is the man who listens to me,
    Watching daily at my gates,
    Waiting at the posts of my doors.
    For whoever finds me finds life,
    And obtains favor from the Lord."

Proverbs 8:32–35

I will go in the strength of the Lord GOD;
    I will make mention of Your righteousness, of
        Yours only.
    O God, You have taught me from my youth;
    And to this day I declare Your wondrous works.
    Now also when I am old and grayheaded,
    O God, do not forsake me,
    Until I declare Your strength to this generation,
    Your power to everyone who is to come.

Psalm 71:16–18

Therefore, laying aside all malice, all deceit, hypocrisy, envy, and all evil speaking, as newborn babes, desire the pure milk of the word, that you may grow thereby.

1 PETER 2:1–2

Teach Your Children to Pray

"And when you pray, you shall not be like the hypocrites. For they love to pray standing in the synagogues and on the corners of the streets, that they may be seen by men. Assuredly, I say to you, they have their reward. But you, when you pray, go into your room, and when you have shut your door, pray to your Father who is in the secret place; and your Father who sees in secret will reward you openly. And when you pray, do not use vain repetitions as the heathen do. For they think that they will be heard for their many words.

"Therefore do not be like them. For your Father knows the things you have need of before you ask Him. In this manner, therefore, pray:

Our Father in heaven,
Hallowed be Your name.

Your kingdom come.
Your will be done
On earth as it is in heaven.
Give us this day our daily bread.
And forgive us our debts,
As we forgive our debtors.
And do not lead us into temptation,
But deliver us from the evil one.
For Yours is the kingdom and the power and the
    glory forever. Amen.

MATTHEW 6:5–13

You shall love the LORD your God with all your heart, with all your soul, and with all your strength. "And these words which I command you today shall be in your heart. You shall teach them diligently to your children, and shall talk of them when you sit in your house, when you walk by the way, when you lie down, and when you rise up."

DEUTERONOMY 6:5–7

So Jesus answered and said to them, "Have faith in God. For assuredly, I say to you, whoever says to this mountain, 'Be removed and be cast into the sea,' and does not doubt in his heart, but believes that those things he says will be done, he will have whatever he says. Therefore I say to you, whatever things you ask when you pray, believe that you receive them, and you will have them.

"And whenever you stand praying, if you have anything against anyone, forgive him, that your Father in heaven may also forgive you your trespasses."

MARK 11:22–25

"Ask, and it will be given to you; seek, and you will find; knock, and it will be opened to you. For everyone who asks receives, and he who seeks finds, and to him who knocks it will be opened."

MATTHEW 7:7–8

Hear me when I call, O God of my righteousness!
    You have relieved me in my distress;
    Have mercy on me, and hear my prayer.

PSALM 4:1

These things I have written to you who believe in the name of the Son of God, that you may know that you have eternal life, and that you may continue to believe in the name of the Son of God.

Now this is the confidence that we have in Him, that if we ask anything according to His will, He hears us. And if we know that He hears us, whatever we ask, we know that we have the petitions that we have asked of Him.

1 John 5:13–15

Be anxious for nothing, but in everything by prayer and supplication, with thanksgiving, let your requests be made known to God; and the peace of God, which surpasses all understanding, will guard your hearts and minds through Christ Jesus.

Philippians 4:6–7

Rejoice always, pray without ceasing, in everything give thanks; for this is the will of God in Christ Jesus for you.

1 Thessalonians 5:16–18

Give heed to the voice of my cry,
    My King and my God,
    For to You I will pray.
    My voice You shall hear in the morning, O
        Lord;
    In the morning I will direct it to You,
    And I will look up.

Psalm 5:2–3

Show Kindness to Your Family

———— ❖ ————

"Yet it shall not be so among you; but whoever desires to become great among you shall be your servant. And whoever of you desires to be first shall be slave of all. For even the Son of Man did not come to be served, but to serve, and to give His life a ransom for many."

MARK 10:43–45

But the fruit of the Spirit is love, joy, peace, longsuffering, kindness, goodness, faithfulness, gentleness, self-control. Against such there is no law.

GALATIANS 5:22–23

Let all bitterness, wrath, anger, clamor, and evil speaking be put away from you, with all malice. And be kind to one another, tenderhearted, forgiving one another, even as God in Christ forgave you.

EPHESIANS 4:31–32

Let love be without hypocrisy. Abhor what is evil. Cling to what is good. Be kindly affectionate to one another with brotherly love, in honor giving preference to one another.

ROMANS 12:9–10

You are witnesses, and God also, how devoutly and justly and blamelessly we behaved ourselves among you who believe; as you know how we exhorted, and comforted, and charged every one of you, as a father does his own children, that you would walk worthy of God who calls you into His own kingdom and glory.

1 THESSALONIANS 2:10–12

"Or what man is there among you who, if his son asks for bread, will give him a stone? Or if he asks for a fish, will he give him a serpent? If you then, being evil, know how to give good gifts to your children, how much more will your Father who is in heaven give good things to those who ask Him!"

MATTHEW 7:9–11

But also for this very reason, giving all diligence, add to your faith virtue, to virtue knowledge, to knowledge self-control, to self-control perseverance, to perseverance godliness, to godliness brotherly kindness, and to brotherly kindness love.

2 Peter 1:5–7

Love suffers long and is kind; love does not envy; love does not parade itself, is not puffed up; does not behave rudely, does not seek its own, is not provoked, thinks no evil; does not rejoice in iniquity, but rejoices in the truth; bears all things, believes all things, hopes all things, endures all things.

1 Corinthians 13:4–7

"For the mountains shall depart
    And the hills be removed,
    But My kindness shall not depart from you,
    Nor shall My covenant of peace be removed,"
    Says the Lord, who has mercy on you.

Isaiah 54:10

Teach Your Children Gratitude

Let your conduct be without covetousness; be content with such things as you have. For He Himself has said, "I will never leave you nor forsake you." So we may boldly say:

> "The LORD is my helper;
>> I will not fear.
>> What can man do to me?"

HEBREWS 13:5–6

Unto the upright there arises light in the
darkness;
He is gracious, and full of compassion, and
righteous.
A good man deals graciously and lends;
He will guide his affairs with discretion.

PSALM 112:4–5

Finally, brethren, whatever things are true, whatever things are noble, whatever things are just, whatever things are pure, whatever things are lovely, whatever things are of good report, if there is any virtue and if there is anything praiseworthy—meditate on these things. The things which you learned and received and heard and saw in me, these do, and the God of peace will be with you.

But I rejoiced in the Lord greatly that now at last your care for me has flourished again; though you surely did care, but you lacked opportunity. Not that I speak in regard to need, for I have learned in whatever state I am, to be content.

PHILIPPIANS 4:8–11

"But now entreat God's favor,
    That He may be gracious to us.
    While this is being done by your hands,
    Will He accept you favorably?"
Says the LORD of hosts.

MALACHI 1:9

Now it happened as He went to Jerusalem that He passed through the midst of Samaria and Galilee. Then as He entered a certain village, there met Him ten men who were lepers, who stood afar off. And they lifted up their voices and said, "Jesus, Master, have mercy on us!"

So when He saw them, He said to them, "Go, show yourselves to the priests." And so it was that as they went, they were cleansed.

And one of them, when he saw that he was healed, returned, and with a loud voice glorified God, and fell down on his face at His feet, giving Him thanks. And he was a Samaritan.

So Jesus answered and said, "Were there not ten cleansed? But where are the nine? Were there not any found who returned to give glory to God except this foreigner?" And He said to him, "Arise, go your way. Your faith has made you well."

LUKE 17:11–19

The words of a wise man's mouth are gracious,
But the lips of a fool shall swallow him up.

ECCLESIASTES 10:12

Sing praise to the LORD, you saints of His,
    And give thanks at the remembrance of His
        holy name.
    For His anger is but for a moment,
    His favor is for life;
    Weeping may endure for a night,
    But joy comes in the morning.
    Now in my prosperity I said,
    "I shall never be moved."

PSALM 30:4–6

Reach Out to Families Who Are Homeless

———— ⋇ ————

But whoever has this world's goods, and sees his brother in need, and shuts up his heart from him, how does the love of God abide in him?

My little children, let us not love in word or in tongue, but in deed and in truth. And by this we know that we are of the truth, and shall assure our hearts before Him.

1 John 3:17–19

And above all things have fervent love for one another, for "love will cover a multitude of sins." Be hospitable to one another without grumbling. As each one has received a gift, minister it to one another, as good stewards of the manifold grace of God.

1 Peter 4:8–10

Happy is he who has the God of Jacob for his help,
Whose hope is in the LORD his God,
Who made heaven and earth,
The sea, and all that is in them;
Who keeps truth forever,
Who executes justice for the oppressed,
Who gives food to the hungry.
The LORD gives freedom to the prisoners.
The LORD opens the eyes of the blind;
The LORD raises those who are bowed down;
The LORD loves the righteous.
The LORD watches over the strangers;
He relieves the fatherless and widow;
But the way of the wicked He turns upside
down.
The LORD shall reign forever—
Your God, O Zion, to all generations.
Praise the LORD!

PSALM 146:5–10

"Is it not to share your bread with the hungry,
And that you bring to your house the poor who
are cast out;
When you see the naked, that you cover him,
And not hide yourself from your own flesh?
Then your light shall break forth like the
morning,
Your healing shall spring forth speedily,
And your righteousness shall go before you;
The glory of the LORD shall be your rear guard.
Then you shall call, and the LORD will answer;
You shall cry, and He will say, 'Here I am.'
"If you take away the yoke from your midst,
The pointing of the finger, and speaking
wickedness,
If you extend your soul to the hungry
And satisfy the afflicted soul,
Then your light shall dawn in the darkness,
And your darkness shall be as the noonday.
The LORD will guide you continually,
And satisfy your soul in drought,
And strengthen your bones;

You shall be like a watered garden,
And like a spring of water, whose waters do
    not fail."

Isaiah 58:7–11

My praise shall be of You in the great assembly;
    I will pay My vows before those who fear Him.
    The poor shall eat and be satisfied;
    Those who seek Him will praise the Lord.
    Let your heart live forever!

Psalm 22:25–26

Blessed is he who considers the poor;
    The Lord will deliver him in time of trouble.
    The Lord will preserve him and keep him alive,
    And he will be blessed on the earth;
    You will not deliver him to the will of his
        enemies.
    The Lord will strengthen him on his bed of
        illness;
    You will sustain him on his sickbed.

Psalm 41:1–3

"When you reap the harvest of your land, you shall not wholly reap the corners of your field, nor shall you gather the gleanings of your harvest. And you shall not glean your vineyard, nor shall you gather every grape of your vineyard; you shall leave them for the poor and the stranger: I am the LORD your God."

LEVITICUS 19:9–10

Love Your Neighbors

———————— ⁎ ————————

"You shall not take vengeance, nor bear any grudge
against the children of your people, but you shall love
your neighbor as yourself: I am the LORD."

LEVITICUS 19:18

Do not withhold good from those to whom it is due,
   When it is in the power of your hand to do so.
   Do not say to your neighbor,
   "Go, and come back,
   And tomorrow I will give it,"
   When you have it with you.
   Do not devise evil against your neighbor,
   For he dwells by you for safety's sake.

PROVERBS 3:27–29

For the commandments, "You shall not commit adultery," "You shall not murder," "You shall not steal," "You shall not bear false witness," "You shall not covet," and if there is any other commandment, are all summed up in this saying, namely, "You shall love your neighbor as yourself." Love does no harm to a neighbor; therefore love is the fulfillment of the law.

ROMANS 13:9–10

For you, brethren, have been called to liberty; only do not use liberty as an opportunity for the flesh, but through love serve one another. For all the law is fulfilled in one word, even in this: "You shall love your neighbor as yourself."

GALATIANS 5:13–14

Jesus said to him, "'You shall love the LORD your God with all your heart, with all your soul, and with all your mind.' This is the first and great commandment. And the second is like it: 'You shall love your neighbor as yourself.' On these two commandments hang all the Law and the Prophets."

MATTHEW 22:37–40

"'Honor your father and your mother,' and, 'You shall love your neighbor as yourself.'"

MATTHEW 19:19

Do not forsake your own friend or your
      father's friend,
    Nor go to your brother's house in the day of
      your calamity;
    Better is a neighbor nearby than a brother
      far away.

PROVERBS 27:10

"You shall not bear false witness against your neighbor.

"You shall not covet your neighbor's house; you shall not covet your neighbor's wife, nor his male servant, nor his female servant, nor his ox, nor his donkey, nor anything that is your neighbor's."

EXODUS 20:16–17

He who despises his neighbor sins;
    But he who has mercy on the poor, happy is he.

PROVERBS 14:21

Whoever secretly slanders his neighbor,
Him I will destroy;
The one who has a haughty look and a
proud heart,
Him I will not endure.
My eyes shall be on the faithful of the land,
That they may dwell with me;
He who walks in a perfect way,
He shall serve me.
He who works deceit shall not dwell within
my house;
He who tells lies shall not continue in my
presence.

Psalm 101:5–7

Comfort Your Children in Their Sorrow

———— ❖ ————

But the mercy of the LORD is from everlasting
     to everlasting
  On those who fear Him,
  And His righteousness to children's children,
  To such as keep His covenant,
  And to those who remember His
    commandments to do them.

PSALM 103:17–18

Blessed be the God and Father of our Lord Jesus
Christ, the Father of mercies and God of all comfort,
who comforts us in all our tribulation, that we may
be able to comfort those who are in any trouble, with
the comfort with which we ourselves are comforted
by God.

2 CORINTHIANS 1:3–4

Behold, the Lord God shall come with a
        strong hand,
    And His arm shall rule for Him;
    Behold, His reward is with Him,
    And His work before Him.
    He will feed His flock like a shepherd;
    He will gather the lambs with His arm,
    And carry them in His bosom,
    And gently lead those who are with young.

Isaiah 40:10–11

Surely He has borne our griefs
    And carried our sorrows;
    Yet we esteemed Him stricken,
    Smitten by God, and afflicted.
    But He was wounded for our transgressions,
    He was bruised for our iniquities;
    The chastisement for our peace was upon Him,
    And by His stripes we are healed.

Isaiah 53:4–5

"Fear not, for I am with you;
　　Be not dismayed, for I am your God.
　　I will strengthen you,
　　Yes, I will help you,
　　I will uphold you with My righteous right
　　　　hand." . . .
　　"Behold, I will make you into a new threshing
　　　　sledge with sharp teeth;
　　You shall thresh the mountains and beat
　　　　them small,
　　And make the hills like chaff.
　　You shall winnow them, the wind shall carry
　　　　them away,
　　And the whirlwind shall scatter them;
　　You shall rejoice in the LORD,
　　And glory in the Holy One of Israel."

ISAIAH 41:10, 15–16

Ask for His Patience

———— ❖ ————

My brethren, count it all joy when you fall into various trials, knowing that the testing of your faith produces patience. But let patience have its perfect work, that you may be perfect and complete, lacking nothing.

JAMES 1:2–4

Therefore we also, since we are surrounded by so great a cloud of witnesses, let us lay aside every weight, and the sin which so easily ensnares us, and let us run with endurance the race that is set before us, looking unto Jesus, the author and finisher of our faith, who for the joy that was set before Him endured the cross, despising the shame, and has sat down at the right hand of the throne of God.

HEBREWS 12:1–2

For whatever things were written before were written for our learning, that we through the patience and comfort of the Scriptures might have hope. Now may the God of patience and comfort grant you to be like-minded toward one another, according to Christ Jesus, that you may with one mind and one mouth glorify the God and Father of our Lord Jesus Christ.

ROMANS 15:4–6

And a servant of the Lord must not quarrel but be gentle to all, able to teach, patient, in humility correcting those who are in opposition, if God perhaps will grant them repentance, so that they may know the truth.

2 TIMOTHY 2:24–25

Now we exhort you, brethren, warn those who are unruly, comfort the fainthearted, uphold the weak, be patient with all. See that no one renders evil for evil to anyone, but always pursue what is good both for yourselves and for all.

1 THESSALONIANS 5:14–15

Therefore, having been justified by faith, we have peace with God through our Lord Jesus Christ, through whom also we have access by faith into this grace in which we stand, and rejoice in hope of the glory of God. And not only that, but we also glory in tribulations, knowing that tribulation produces perseverance; and perseverance, character; and character, hope.

ROMANS 5:1–4

But, beloved, we are confident of better things concerning you, yes, things that accompany salvation, though we speak in this manner. For God is not unjust to forget your work and labor of love which you have shown toward His name, in that you have ministered to the saints, and do minister. And we desire that each one of you show the same diligence to the full assurance of hope until the end, that you do not become sluggish, but imitate those who through faith and patience inherit the promises.

HEBREWS 6:9–12

We give thanks to God always for you all, making mention of you in our prayers, remembering without ceasing your work of faith, labor of love, and patience of hope in our Lord Jesus Christ in the sight of our God and Father, knowing, beloved brethren, your election by God. For our gospel did not come to you in word only, but also in power, and in the Holy Spirit and in much assurance, as you know what kind of men we were among you for your sake.

1 Thessalonians 1:2–5

The end of a thing is better than its beginning;
    The patient in spirit is better than the proud
        in spirit.

Ecclesiastes 7:8

Do not grumble against one another, brethren, lest you be condemned. Behold, the Judge is standing at the door! My brethren, take the prophets, who spoke in the name of the Lord, as an example of suffering and patience. Indeed we count them blessed who endure.

James 5:9–11

Seek His Spirit's Guidance

———————— ❖ ————————

Teach me to do Your will,
>   For You are my God;
>   Your Spirit is good.
>   Lead me in the land of uprightness.
>   Revive me, O Lord, for Your name's sake!
>   For Your righteousness' sake bring my soul out
>   of trouble.

PSALM 143:10–11

Now the Lord is the Spirit; and where the Spirit of the
Lord is, there is liberty. But we all, with unveiled face,
beholding as in a mirror the glory of the Lord, are
being transformed into the same image from glory to
glory, just as by the Spirit of the Lord.

2 CORINTHIANS 3:17–18

I say then: Walk in the Spirit, and you shall not fulfill the lust of the flesh. For the flesh lusts against the Spirit, and the Spirit against the flesh; and these are contrary to one another, so that you do not do the things that you wish. But if you are led by the Spirit, you are not under the law.

Now the works of the flesh are evident, which are: adultery, fornication, uncleanness, lewdness, idolatry, sorcery, hatred, contentions, jealousies, outbursts of wrath, selfish ambitions, dissensions, heresies, envy, murders, drunkenness, revelries, and the like; of which I tell you beforehand, just as I also told you in time past, that those who practice such things will not inherit the kingdom of God.

But the fruit of the Spirit is love, joy, peace, longsuffering, kindness, goodness, faithfulness, gentleness, self-control. Against such there is no law. And those who are Christ's have crucified the flesh with its passions and desires. If we live in the Spirit, let us also walk in the Spirit. Let us not become conceited, provoking one another, envying one another.

GALATIANS 5:16–26

No one has seen God at any time. If we love one another, God abides in us, and His love has been perfected in us. By this we know that we abide in Him, and He in us, because He has given us of His Spirit.

1 John 4:12–13

Do you not know that you are the temple of God and that the Spirit of God dwells in you? If anyone defiles the temple of God, God will destroy him. For the temple of God is holy, which temple you are.

1 Corinthians 3:16–17

"However, when He, the Spirit of truth, has come, He will guide you into all truth; for He will not speak on His own authority, but whatever He hears He will speak; and He will tell you things to come. He will glorify Me, for He will take of what is Mine and declare it to you. All things that the Father has are Mine. Therefore I said that He will take of Mine and declare it to you."

John 16:13–15

But God has revealed them to us through His Spirit. For the Spirit searches all things, yes, the deep things of God. For what man knows the things of a man except the spirit of the man which is in him? Even so no one knows the things of God except the Spirit of God. Now we have received, not the spirit of the world, but the Spirit who is from God, that we might know the things that have been freely given to us by God.

These things we also speak, not in words which man's wisdom teaches but which the Holy Spirit teaches, comparing spiritual things with spiritual. But the natural man does not receive the things of the Spirit of God, for they are foolishness to him; nor can he know them, because they are spiritually discerned. But he who is spiritual judges all things, yet he himself is rightly judged by no one. For "who has known the mind of the LORD that he may instruct Him?" But we have the mind of Christ.

1 CORINTHIANS 2:10–16

And we have such trust through Christ toward God. Not that we are sufficient of ourselves to think of anything as being from ourselves, but our sufficiency is from God, who also made us sufficient as ministers of the new covenant, not of the letter but of the Spirit; for the letter kills, but the Spirit gives life.

2 Corinthians 3:4–6

Admit Your Shortcomings
as a Father

———— ❖ ————

O God, do not be far from me;
    O my God, make haste to help me! . . .

    My mouth shall tell of Your righteousness
    And Your salvation all the day,
    For I do not know their limits.
    I will go in the strength of the Lord GOD;
    I will make mention of Your righteousness, of
        Yours only.
    O God, You have taught me from my youth;
    And to this day I declare Your wondrous works.
    Now also when I am old and grayheaded,
    O God, do not forsake me,
    Until I declare Your strength to this generation,
    Your power to everyone who is to come.

PSALM 71:12, 15–18

Oh, love the LORD, all you His saints!
  For the LORD preserves the faithful,
  And fully repays the proud person.
  Be of good courage,
  And He shall strengthen your heart,
  All you who hope in the LORD.

PSALM 31:23–24

"For I will pour water on him who is thirsty,
  And floods on the dry ground;
  I will pour My Spirit on your descendants,
  And My blessing on your offspring;
  They will spring up among the grass
  Like willows by the watercourses."

ISAIAH 44:3–4

So then neither he who plants is anything, nor he who waters, but God who gives the increase. Now he who plants and he who waters are one, and each one will receive his own reward according to his own labor.

For we are God's fellow workers; you are God's field, you are God's building.

1 CORINTHIANS 3:7–9

Only take heed to yourself, and diligently keep yourself, lest you forget the things your eyes have seen, and lest they depart from your heart all the days of your life. And teach them to your children and your grandchildren, especially concerning the day you stood before the Lord your God in Horeb, when the Lord said to me, "Gather the people to Me, and I will let them hear My words, that they may learn to fear Me all the days they live on the earth, and that they may teach their children."

DEUTERONOMY 4:9–10

Now it shall come to pass, if you diligently obey the voice of the Lord your God, to observe carefully all His commandments which I command you today, that the Lord your God will set you high above all nations of the earth. . . . Blessed shall be the fruit of your body, the produce of your ground and the increase of your herds, the increase of your cattle and the offspring of your flocks.

DEUTERONOMY 28:1, 4

The way of the lazy man is like a hedge of thorns,

But the way of the upright is a highway.
A wise son makes a father glad,
But a foolish man despises his mother.
Folly is joy to him who is destitute of
    discernment,
But a man of understanding walks uprightly.
Without counsel, plans go awry,
But in the multitude of counselors they are
    established.
A man has joy by the answer of his mouth,
And a word spoken in due season, how good it
    is!
The way of life winds upward for the wise,
That he may turn away from hell below.
The LORD will destroy the house of the proud,
But He will establish the boundary of the
    widow.
The thoughts of the wicked are an abomination
    to the LORD,
But the words of the pure are pleasant.

He who is greedy for gain troubles his own
    house,
But he who hates bribes will live.
The heart of the righteous studies how to
    answer,
But the mouth of the wicked pours forth evil.
The LORD is far from the wicked,
But He hears the prayer of the righteous.
The light of the eyes rejoices the heart,
And a good report makes the bones healthy.
The ear that hears the rebukes of life
Will abide among the wise.
He who disdains instruction despises his own
    soul,
But he who heeds rebuke gets understanding.
The fear of the LORD is the instruction of
    wisdom,
And before honor is humility.

PROVERBS 15:19–33

The LORD is good,
    A stronghold in the day of trouble;
    And He knows those who trust in Him.

NAHUM 1:7

Have the Courage to Be a
Man of Integrity

He who speaks truth declares righteousness,
But a false witness, deceit.
There is one who speaks like the piercings of a
sword,
But the tongue of the wise promotes health.
The truthful lip shall be established forever,
But a lying tongue is but for a moment.

PROVERBS 12:17–19

I will behave wisely in a perfect way.
Oh, when will You come to me?
I will walk within my house with a perfect heart.

PSALM 101:2

Blessed is the man
    Who walks not in the counsel of the ungodly,
        Nor stands in the path of sinners,
        Nor sits in the seat of the scornful;
    But his delight is in the law of the Lord,
        And in His law he meditates day and night.
    He shall be like a tree
        Planted by the rivers of water,
        That brings forth its fruit in its season,
        Whose leaf also shall not wither;
    And whatever he does shall prosper.

The ungodly are not so,
But are like the chaff which the wind drives
    away.
Therefore the ungodly shall not stand in the
    judgment,
Nor sinners in the congregation of the righteous.

For the Lord knows the way of the righteous,
But the way of the ungodly shall perish.

Psalm 1:1–6

The Lord shall judge the peoples;
  Judge me, O Lord, according to my
    righteousness,
  And according to my integrity within me.

Psalm 7:8

Blessed are the undefiled in the way,
  Who walk in the law of the Lord!
  Blessed are those who keep His testimonies,
  Who seek Him with the whole heart!
  They also do no iniquity;
  They walk in His ways.
  You have commanded us
  To keep Your precepts diligently.
  Oh, that my ways were directed
  To keep Your statutes!
  Then I would not be ashamed,
  When I look into all Your commandments.
  I will praise You with uprightness of heart,
  When I learn Your righteous judgments.
  I will keep Your statutes;
  Oh, do not forsake me utterly!

Psalm 119:1–8

Keep my soul, and deliver me;
>Let me not be ashamed, for I put my trust in
>>You.
>Let integrity and uprightness preserve me,
>For I wait for You.

Psalm 25:20–21

Dishonest scales are an abomination to the Lord,
>But a just weight is His delight.

>When pride comes, then comes shame;
>But with the humble is wisdom.

>The integrity of the upright will guide them,
>But the perversity of the unfaithful will destroy
>>them.

Proverbs 11:1–3

Diverse weights are an abomination to the Lord,
>And dishonest scales are not good.

Proverbs 20:23

A good man deals graciously and lends;
>   He will guide his affairs with discretion.
>   Surely he will never be shaken;
>   The righteous will be in everlasting
>   remembrance.
>   He will not be afraid of evil tidings;
>   His heart is steadfast, trusting in the Lord.

Psalm 112:5–7

Better is the poor who walks in his integrity
>   Than one who is perverse in his lips, and is a
>   fool.

Proverbs 19:1

GOD LISTENS
TO YOUR
PRAYERS
WHEN . . .

You Seek His Wisdom for Your Children

The days of our lives are seventy years;
    And if by reason of strength they are eighty
        years,
    Yet their boast is only labor and sorrow;
    For it is soon cut off, and we fly away.
    Who knows the power of Your anger?
    For as the fear of You, so is Your wrath.
    So teach us to number our days,
    That we may gain a heart of wisdom.

PSALM 90:10–12

My son, pay attention to my wisdom;
    Lend your ear to my understanding,
    That you may preserve discretion,
    And your lips may keep knowledge.

PROVERBS 5:1–2

She is more precious than rubies,
    And all the things you may desire cannot
        compare with her.
    Length of days is in her right hand,
    In her left hand riches and honor.
    Her ways are ways of pleasantness,
    And all her paths are peace.
    She is a tree of life to those who take hold of her,
    And happy are all who retain her.

The LORD by wisdom founded the earth;
By understanding He established the heavens;
By His knowledge the depths were broken up,
And clouds drop down the dew.
My son, let them not depart from your eyes—
Keep sound wisdom and discretion;
So they will be life to your soul
And grace to your neck.

PROVERBS 3:15–22

The fear of the LORD is the beginning of wisdom;
   A good understanding have all those who do
      His commandments.
   His praise endures forever.

PSALM 111:10

If any of you lacks wisdom, let him ask of God, who gives to all liberally and without reproach, and it will be given to him. But let him ask in faith, with no doubting, for he who doubts is like a wave of the sea driven and tossed by the wind.

JAMES 1:5–6

How much better to get wisdom than gold!
   And to get understanding is to be chosen rather
      than silver.
   The highway of the upright is to depart
      from evil;
   He who keeps his way preserves his soul.

PROVERBS 16:16–17

But the wisdom that is from above is first pure, then peaceable, gentle, willing to yield, full of mercy and good fruits, without partiality and without hypocrisy.

JAMES 3:17

"Get wisdom! Get understanding!
    Do not forget, nor turn away from the words of
      my mouth.
    Do not forsake her, and she will preserve you;
    Love her, and she will keep you.
    Wisdom is the principal thing;
    Therefore get wisdom.
    And in all your getting, get understanding.
    Exalt her, and she will promote you;
    She will bring you honor, when you embrace her.
    She will place on your head an ornament of grace;
    A crown of glory she will deliver to you."

Hear, my son, and receive my sayings,
And the years of your life will be many.
I have taught you in the way of wisdom;
I have led you in right paths.

PROVERBS 4:5–11

You Are Overwhelmed with Your Family Responsibilities

———⚜———

"Fear not, for I have redeemed you;
    I have called you by your name;
    You are Mine.
    When you pass through the waters, I will be
        with you;
    And through the rivers, they shall not overflow
        you.
    When you walk through the fire, you shall not
        be burned,
    Nor shall the flame scorch you.
    For I am the LORD your God,
    The Holy One of Israel, your Savior.

ISAIAH 43:1–3

Unless the LORD builds the house,
    They labor in vain who build it;
    Unless the LORD guards the city,
    The watchman stays awake in vain.
    It is vain for you to rise up early,
    To sit up late,
    To eat the bread of sorrows;
    For so He gives His beloved sleep.

    Behold, children are a heritage from the LORD,
    The fruit of the womb is a reward.
    Like arrows in the hand of a warrior,
    So are the children of one's youth.
    Happy is the man who has his quiver full of them;
    They shall not be ashamed,
    But shall speak with their enemies in the gate.

PSALM 127:1–5

"For the mountains shall depart
    And the hills be removed,
    But My kindness shall not depart from you,
    Nor shall My covenant of peace be removed,"
    Says the LORD, who has mercy on you.

ISAIAH 54:10

I cried out to God with my voice—
> To God with my voice;
> And He gave ear to me.
> In the day of my trouble I sought the Lord;
> My hand was stretched out in the night without
>> ceasing;
> My soul refused to be comforted.
> I remembered God, and was troubled;
> I complained, and my spirit was overwhelmed.
>> Selah . . .
> Will the Lord cast off forever?
> And will He be favorable no more?
> Has His mercy ceased forever?
> Has His promise failed forevermore?
> Has God forgotten to be gracious?
> Has He in anger shut up His tender mercies?
>> Selah
> And I said, "This is my anguish;
> But I will remember the years of the right hand
>> of the Most High."
> I will remember the works of the LORD;
> Surely I will remember Your wonders of old.
> I will also meditate on all Your work,

And talk of Your deeds.
Your way, O God, is in the sanctuary;
Who is so great a God as our God?

PSALM 77:1–3, 7–13

Trust in the LORD with all your heart,
And lean not on your own understanding;
In all your ways acknowledge Him,
And He shall direct your paths.
Do not be wise in your own eyes;
Fear the LORD and depart from evil.

PROVERBS 3:5–7

Therefore, brethren, stand fast and hold the traditions which you were taught, whether by word or our epistle.

Now may our Lord Jesus Christ Himself, and our God and Father, who has loved us and given us everlasting consolation and good hope by grace, comfort your hearts and establish you in every good word and work.

2 THESSALONIANS 2:15–17

Have you not known? Have you not heard? The ever-lasting God, the LORD, the Creator of the ends of the earth, neither faints nor is weary. His understanding is unsearchable. He gives power to the weak, and to the those who have no might He increases strength.

ISAIAH 40:28–31

I can do all things through Christ who gives me strength.

PHILIPPIANS 4:13

Commit your way to the LORD,
　　Trust also in Him,
　　And He shall bring it to pass.

PSALM 37:5

You Seek His Forgiveness When You Wrong Your Family

"For if you forgive men their trespasses, your heavenly Father will also forgive you. But if you do not forgive men their trespasses, neither will your Father forgive your trespasses."

MATTHEW 6:14–15

A man's pride will bring him low,
    But the humble in spirit will retain honor.

PROVERBS 29:23

"And whenever you stand praying, if you have anything against anyone, forgive him, that your Father in heaven may also forgive you your trespasses. But if you do not forgive, neither will your Father in heaven forgive your trespasses."

MARK 11:25–26

Bless the Lord, O my soul;
    And all that is within me, bless His holy name!
    Bless the Lord, O my soul,
    And forget not all His benefits:
    Who forgives all your iniquities,
    Who heals all your diseases,
    Who redeems your life from destruction,
    Who crowns you with lovingkindness and
        tender mercies,
    Who satisfies your mouth with good things,
    So that your youth is renewed like the eagle's.

PSALM 103:1–5

If You, Lord, should mark iniquities,
    O Lord, who could stand?
    But there is forgiveness with You,
    That You may be feared.

PSALM 130:3–4

He who covers his sins will not prosper,
    But whoever confesses and forsakes them will
        have mercy.

PROVERBS 28:13

Take heed to yourselves. If your brother sins against you, rebuke him; and if he repents, forgive him. And if he sins against you seven times in a day, and seven times in a day returns to you, saying, 'I repent,' you shall forgive him."

Luke 17:3–4

As the elect of God, holy and beloved, put on tender mercies, kindness, humility, meekness, longsuffering; bearing with one another, and forgiving one another, if anyone has a complaint against another; even as Christ forgave you, so you also must do.

Colossians 3:12–13

I, therefore, the prisoner of the Lord, beseech you to walk worthy of the calling with which you were called, with all lowliness and gentleness, with longsuffering, bearing with one another in love, endeavoring to keep the unity of the Spirit in the bond of peace.

Ephesians 4:1–3

You Feel Depressed and Lose Your Way

⁕

The righteous cry out, and the LORD hears,
> And delivers them out of all their troubles.
> The LORD is near to those who have a broken
> heart,
> And saves such as have a contrite spirit.

> Many are the afflictions of the righteous,
> But the LORD delivers him out of them all.

PSALM 34:17–19

Beloved, do not think it strange concerning the fiery trial which is to try you, as though some strange thing happened to you; but rejoice to the extent that you partake of Christ's sufferings, that when His glory is revealed, you may also be glad with exceeding joy.

1 PETER 4:12–13

Blessed be the God and Father of our Lord Jesus Christ, the Father of mercies and God of all comfort, who comforts us in all our tribulation, that we may be able to comfort those who are in any trouble, with the comfort with which we ourselves are comforted by God.

2 CORINTHIANS 1:3–4

Finally, brethren, whatever things are true, whatever things are noble, whatever things are just, whatever things are pure, whatever things are lovely, whatever things are of good report, if there is any virtue and if there is anything praiseworthy—meditate on these things.

PHILIPPIANS 4:8

Therefore humble yourselves under the mighty hand of God, that He may exalt you in due time, casting all your care upon Him, for He cares for you.

1 PETER 5:6–7

Then he said to them, "Go your way, eat the fat, drink the sweet, and send portions to those for whom nothing is prepared; for this day is holy to our Lord. Do not sorrow, for the joy of the Lord is your strength."

NEHEMIAH 8:10

For I am persuaded that neither death nor life, nor angels nor principalities nor powers, nor things present nor things to come, nor height nor depth, nor any other created thing, shall be able to separate us from the love of God which is in Christ Jesus our Lord.

ROMANS 8:38–39

The Lord builds up Jerusalem;
    He gathers together the outcasts of Israel.
    He heals the brokenhearted
    And binds up their wounds.
    He counts the number of the stars;
    He calls them all by name.
    Great is our Lord, and mighty in power;
    His understanding is infinite.
    The Lord lifts up the humble;
    He casts the wicked down to the ground.

PSALM 147:2–6

Your Children Disappoint You

———— ✣ ————

Better is a dry morsel with quietness,
    Than a house full of feasting with strife.
    A wise servant will rule over a son who causes
        shame,
    And will share an inheritance among the
        brothers.

PROVERBS 17:1–2

Those who are planted in the house of the LORD
    Shall flourish in the courts of our God.
    They shall still bear fruit in old age;
    They shall be fresh and flourishing,
    To declare that the LORD is upright;
    He is my rock, and there is no
        unrighteousness in Him.

PSALM 92:13–15

"Lift up your eyes to the heavens,
	And look on the earth beneath.
	For the heavens will vanish away like smoke,
	The earth will grow old like a garment,
	And those who dwell in it will die in like manner;
	But My salvation will be forever,
	And My righteousness will not be abolished.
	"Listen to Me, you who know righteousness,
	You people in whose heart is My law:
	Do not fear the reproach of men,
	Nor be afraid of their insults." . . .
	Awake, awake, put on strength,
	O arm of the LORD!
	Awake as in the ancient days,
	In the generations of old.
	Are You not the arm that cut Rahab apart,
	And wounded the serpent?
	Are You not the One who dried up the sea,
	The waters of the great deep;
	That made the depths of the sea a road
	For the redeemed to cross over?
	So the ransomed of the LORD shall return,

And come to Zion with singing,
With everlasting joy on their heads.
They shall obtain joy and gladness;
Sorrow and sighing shall flee away.

ISAIAH 51:6–7, 9–11

And let us not grow weary while doing good, for in due season we shall reap if we do not lose heart.

GALATIANS 6:9

For I know of nothing against myself, yet I am not justified by this; but He who judges me is the Lord. Therefore judge nothing before the time, until the Lord comes, who will both bring to light the hidden things of darkness and reveal the counsels of the hearts. Then each one's praise will come from God.

1 CORINTHIANS 4:4–5

"For a mere moment I have forsaken you,
But with great mercies I will gather you. . . .
All your children shall be taught by the LORD,
And great shall be the peace of your children."

ISAIAH 54:7, 13

For the LORD will not cast off His people,
　　Nor will He forsake His inheritance.
　　But judgment will return to righteousness,
　　And all the upright in heart will follow it.

PSALM 94:14–15

In this you greatly rejoice, though now for a little while, if need be, you have been grieved by various trials, that the genuineness of your faith, being much more precious than gold that perishes, though it is tested by fire, may be found to praise, honor, and glory at the revelation of Jesus Christ, whom having not seen you love. Though now you do not see Him, yet believing, you rejoice with joy inexpressible and full of glory, receiving the end of your faith—the salvation of your souls.

1 PETER 1:6–9

Therefore do not cast away your confidence, which has great reward. For you have need of endurance, so that after you have done the will of God, you may receive the promise.

HEBREWS 10:35–36

You Trust Him Even When You Don't Understand

In the day of my trouble I will call upon You,
For You will answer me.
Among the gods there is none like You, O Lord;
Nor are there any works like Your works.
All nations whom You have made
Shall come and worship before You, O Lord,
And shall glorify Your name.
For You are great, and do wondrous things;
You alone are God.

PSALM 86:7–10

Every word of God is pure;
He is a shield to those who put their trust in Him.

PROVERBS 30:5

Brethren, in all our affliction and distress we were comforted concerning you by your faith. For now we live, if you stand fast in the Lord.

1 Thessalonians 3:7–8

Then they cried out to the Lord in their trouble,
>And He saved them out of their distresses.
>He sent His word and healed them,
>And delivered them from their destructions.

Psalm 107:19–20

Behold, He who keeps Israel
>Shall neither slumber nor sleep.
>The Lord is your keeper;
>The Lord is your shade at your right hand.
>The sun shall not strike you by day,
>Nor the moon by night.
>The Lord shall preserve you from all evil;
>He shall preserve your soul.
>The Lord shall preserve your going out and
>>your coming in
>
>From this time forth, and even forevermore.

Psalm 121:4–8

You Trust Him When You Wait for His Answers

For since the beginning of the world
  Men have not heard nor perceived by the ear,
  Nor has the eye seen any God besides You,
  Who acts for the one who waits for Him.
  You meet him who rejoices and does
    righteousness,
  Who remembers You in Your ways.

Isaiah 64:4–5

The LORD your God in your midst,
  The Mighty One, will save;
  He will rejoice over you with gladness,
  He will quiet you with His love,
  He will rejoice over you with singing.

Zephaniah 3:17

I waited patiently for the Lord;
 And He inclined to me,
 And heard my cry.
 He also brought me up out of a horrible pit,
 Out of the miry clay,
 And set my feet upon a rock,
 And established my steps.
 He has put a new song in my mouth—
 Praise to our God;
 Many will see it and fear,
 And will trust in the Lord.

Psalm 40:1–3

Every word of God is pure;
 He is a shield to those who put their trust in Him.

Proverbs 30:5

But those who wait on the Lord
 Shall renew their strength;
 They shall mount up with wings like eagles,
 They shall run and not be weary,
 They shall walk and not faint.

Isaiah 40:31

My soul, wait silently for God alone,
    For my expectation is from Him.
    He only is my rock and my salvation;
    He is my defense;
    I shall not be moved.
    In God is my salvation and my glory;
    The rock of my strength,
    And my refuge, is in God.
    Trust in Him at all times, you people;
    Pour out your heart before Him;
    God is a refuge for us.

PSALM 62:5–8

Be anxious for nothing, but in everything by prayer and supplication, with thanksgiving, let your requests be made known to God; and the peace of God, which surpasses all understanding, will guard your hearts and minds through Christ Jesus.

PHILIPPIANS 4:6–7

Do not be deceived, my beloved brethren. Every good gift and every perfect gift is from above, and comes down from the Father of lights, with whom there is no variation or shadow of turning.

JAMES 1:16–17

Trust in the LORD, and do good;
    Dwell in the land, and feed on His faithfulness.
    Delight yourself also in the LORD,
    And He shall give you the desires of your heart.
    Commit your way to the LORD,
    Trust also in Him,
    And He shall bring it to pass.
    He shall bring forth your righteousness as the
        light,
    And your justice as the noonday.
    Rest in the LORD, and wait patiently for Him.

PSALM 37:3–7

You Claim Victory Over the Sins in Your Life

———————⁂———————

Therefore, if anyone is in Christ, he is a new creation; old things have passed away; behold, all things have become new. Now all things are of God, who has reconciled us to Himself through Jesus Christ, and has given us the ministry of reconciliation, that is, that God was in Christ reconciling the world to Himself, not imputing their trespasses to them, and has committed to us the word of reconciliation.

Now then, we are ambassadors for Christ, as though God were pleading through us: we implore you on Christ's behalf, be reconciled to God. For He made Him who knew no sin to be sin for us, that we might become the righteousness of God in Him.

2 CORINTHIANS 5:17–21

Therefore, since we have this ministry, as we have received mercy, we do not lose heart. But we have renounced the hidden things of shame, not walking in craftiness nor handling the word of God deceitfully, but by manifestation of the truth commending ourselves to every man's conscience in the sight of God. But even if our gospel is veiled, it is veiled to those who are perishing, whose minds the god of this age has blinded, who do not believe, lest the light of the gospel of the glory of Christ, who is the image of God, should shine on them. For we do not preach ourselves, but Christ Jesus the Lord, and ourselves your bondservants for Jesus' sake. For it is the God who commanded light to shine out of darkness, who has shone in our hearts to give the light of the knowledge of the glory of God in the face of Jesus Christ.

2 CORINTHIANS 4:1–6

Stand fast therefore in the liberty by which Christ has made us free, and do not be entangled again with a yoke of bondage.

GALATIANS 5:1

"Learn to do good;
    Seek justice,
    Rebuke the oppressor;
    Defend the fatherless,
    Plead for the widow.
    "Come now, and let us reason together,"
    Says the LORD,
    "Though your sins are like scarlet,
    They shall be as white as snow;
    Though they are red like crimson,
    They shall be as wool.
    If you are willing and obedient,
    You shall eat the good of the land."

ISAIAH 1:17–19

O God, You know my foolishness;
    And my sins are not hidden from You.
    Let not those who wait for You, O Lord GOD of
        hosts, be ashamed because of me;
    Let not those who seek You be confounded
        because of me, O God of Israel.

PSALM 69:5–6

Finally, my brethren, be strong in the Lord and in the power of His might. Put on the whole armor of God, that you may be able to stand against the wiles of the devil. For we do not wrestle against flesh and blood, but against principalities, against powers, against the rulers of the darkness of this age, against spiritual hosts of wickedness in the heavenly places. Therefore take up the whole armor of God, that you may be able to withstand in the evil day, and having done all, to stand.

Stand therefore, having girded your waist with truth, having put on the breastplate of righteousness, and having shod your feet with the preparation of the gospel of peace; above all, taking the shield of faith with which you will be able to quench all the fiery darts of the wicked one. And take the helmet of salvation, and the sword of the Spirit, which is the word of God; praying always with all prayer and supplication in the Spirit, being watchful to this end with all perseverance and supplication for all the saints.

Ephesians 6:10–18

This is the message which we have heard from Him and declare to you, that God is light and in Him is no darkness at all. If we say that we have fellowship with Him, and walk in darkness, we lie and do not practice the truth. But if we walk in the light as He is in the light, we have fellowship with one another, and the blood of Jesus Christ His Son cleanses us from all sin.

If we say that we have no sin, we deceive ourselves, and the truth is not in us. If we confess our sins, He is faithful and just to forgive us our sins and to cleanse us from all unrighteousness. If we say that we have not sinned, we make Him a liar, and His word is not in us.

1 John 1:5–10

"O Death, where is your sting?
O Hades, where is your victory?"

The sting of death is sin, and the strength of sin is the law. But thanks be to God, who gives us the victory through our Lord Jesus Christ.

Therefore, my beloved brethren, be steadfast, immovable, always abounding in the work of the Lord, knowing that your labor is not in vain in the Lord.

1 Corinthians 15:55–58

You Dedicate Your Life to Christ

———— ❧ ————

Though the fig tree may not blossom,
    Nor fruit be on the vines;
    Though the labor of the olive may fail,
    And the fields yield no food;
    Though the flock may be cut off from the fold,
    And there be no herd in the stalls—
    Yet I will rejoice in the Lord,
    I will joy in the God of my salvation.
    The Lord God is my strength;
    He will make my feet like deer's feet,
    And He will make me walk on my high hills.

Habakkuk 3:17–19

The Lord is my light and my salvation;
Whom shall I fear?
The Lord is the strength of my life;
Of whom shall I be afraid?
When the wicked came against me
To eat up my flesh,
My enemies and foes,
They stumbled and fell.
Though an army may encamp against me,
My heart shall not fear;
Though war may rise against me,
In this I will be confident.

Psalm 27:1–3

The Lord is my strength and my shield;
My heart trusted in Him, and I am helped;
Therefore my heart greatly rejoices,
And with my song I will praise Him.
The Lord is their strength,
And He is the saving refuge of His anointed.

Psalm 28:7–8

Now therefore, fear the LORD, serve Him in sincerity and in truth, and put away the gods which your fathers served on the other side of the River and in Egypt. Serve the LORD! And if it seems evil to you to serve the LORD, choose for yourselves this day whom you will serve, whether the gods which your fathers served that were on the other side of the River, or the gods of the Amorites, in whose land you dwell. But as for me and my house, we will serve the LORD.

JOSHUA 24:14–15

How much more shall the blood of Christ, who through the eternal Spirit offered Himself without spot to God, cleanse your conscience from dead works to serve the living God? And for this reason He is the Mediator of the new covenant, by means of death, for the redemption of the transgressions under the first covenant, that those who are called may receive the promise of the eternal inheritance.

HEBREWS 9:14–15

As for God, His way is perfect;
    The word of the LORD is proven;
    He is a shield to all who trust in Him.
    For who is God, except the LORD?
    And who is a rock, except our God?
    It is God who arms me with strength,
    And makes my way perfect.
    He makes my feet like the feet of deer,
    And sets me on my high places.

PSALM 18:30–33

But the Lord is faithful, who will establish you and guard you from the evil one. And we have confidence in the Lord concerning you, both that you do and will do the things we command you.

Now may the Lord direct your hearts into the love of God and into the patience of Christ.

2 THESSALONIANS 3:3–5

And this is the testimony: that God has given us eternal life, and this life is in His Son. He who has the Son has life; he who does not have the Son of God does not have life. These things I have written to you who believe in the name of the Son of God, that you may know that you have eternal life, and that you may continue to believe in the name of the Son of God.

Now this is the confidence that we have in Him, that if we ask anything according to His will, He hears us. And if we know that He hears us, whatever we ask, we know that we have the petitions that we have asked of Him.

1 John 5:11–15

Serve the Lord with gladness;
> Come before His presence with singing.
> Know that the Lord, He is God;
> It is He who has made us, and not we ourselves;
> We are His people and the sheep of His pasture.

Psalm 100:2–3

GOD'S SPECIAL
LOVE IS WITH
YOU WHEN . . .

You Bring Problems to Him

"For the eyes of the LORD are on the righteous,
    And His ears are open to their prayers;
    But the face of the LORD is against those who
        do evil."
    And who is he who will harm you if you become
followers of what is good? But even if you should suffer for righteousness' sake, you are blessed. "And do not be afraid of their threats, nor be troubled." But sanctify the Lord God in your hearts, and always be ready to give a defense to everyone who asks you a reason for the hope that is in you, with meekness and fear.

1 PETER 3:12–15

But Jesus looked at them and said to them, "With men this is impossible, but with God all things are possible."

MATTHEW 19:26

"The Spirit of the Lord God is upon Me,
Because the Lord has anointed Me
To preach good tidings to the poor;
He has sent Me to heal the brokenhearted,
To proclaim liberty to the captives,
And the opening of the prison to those who are
bound;
To proclaim the acceptable year of the Lord,
And the day of vengeance of our God;
To comfort all who mourn,
To console those who mourn in Zion,
To give them beauty for ashes,
The oil of joy for mourning,
The garment of praise for the spirit of heaviness;
That they may be called trees of righteousness,
The planting of the Lord, that He may be
glorified."

Isaiah 61:1–3

If you would prepare your heart,
    And stretch out your hands toward Him;
    If iniquity were in your hand, and you put it
        far away,
    And would not let wickedness dwell in your
        tents;
    Then surely you could lift up your face without
        spot;
    Yes, you could be steadfast, and not fear;
    Because you would forget your misery,
    And remember it as waters that have passed
        away,
    And your life would be brighter than noonday.
    Though you were dark, you would be like the
        morning.
    And you would be secure, because there is hope;
    Yes, you would dig around you, and take your
        rest in safety.

JOB 11:13–18

Yes, we had the sentence of death in ourselves, that we should not trust in ourselves but in God who raises the dead, who delivered us from so great a death, and does deliver us; in whom we trust that He will still deliver us.

2 CORINTHIANS 1:9–10

Consider what I say, and may the Lord give you understanding in all things. . . .

This is a faithful saying:

For if we died with Him,

We shall also live with Him.

If we endure,

We shall also reign with Him.

If we deny Him,

He also will deny us.

2 TIMOTHY 2:7, 11–12

We are hard-pressed on every side, yet not crushed; we are perplexed, but not in despair; persecuted, but not forsaken; struck down, but not destroyed— always carrying about in the body the dying of the Lord Jesus, that the life of Jesus also may be manifested in our body. . . .

For all things are for your sakes, that grace, having spread through the many, may cause thanksgiving to abound to the glory of God.

Therefore we do not lose heart. Even though our outward man is perishing, yet the inward man is being renewed day by day. For our light affliction, which is but for a moment, is working for us a far more exceeding and eternal weight of glory, while we do not look at the things which are seen, but at the things which are not seen. For the things which are seen are temporary, but the things which are not seen are eternal.

2 CORINTHIANS 4:8–10, 15–18

You Rely on Him to Guide and Direct Your Children

———— ⚹ ————

When you roam, they will lead you;
>   When you sleep, they will keep you;
>   And when you awake, they will speak with you.
>   For the commandment is a lamp,
>   And the law a light;
>   Reproofs of instruction are the way of life.

PROVERBS 6:22–23

"I, the LORD, have called You in righteousness,
>   And will hold Your hand;
>   I will keep You and give You as a covenant to the
>   people,
>   As a light to the Gentiles."

ISAIAH 42:6

Have you not known?
　　Have you not heard?
　　The everlasting God, the Lord,
　　The Creator of the ends of the earth,
　　Neither faints nor is weary.
　　His understanding is unsearchable.
　　He gives power to the weak,
　　And to those who have no might He increases
　　　　strength.
　　Even the youths shall faint and be weary,
　　And the young men shall utterly fall,
　　But those who wait on the Lord
　　Shall renew their strength;
　　They shall mount up with wings like eagles,
　　They shall run and not be weary,
　　They shall walk and not faint.

Isaiah 40:28–31

Trust in the Lord with all your heart,
　　And lean not on your own understanding;
　　In all your ways acknowledge Him,
　　And He shall direct your paths.

Proverbs 3:5–6

"Fear not, for I am with you;
    Be not dismayed, for I am your God.
    I will strengthen you,
    Yes, I will help you,
    I will uphold you with My righteous right hand."

ISAIAH 41:10

A man's heart plans his way,
    But the LORD directs his steps.

PROVERBS 16:9

"Do not remember the former things,
    Nor consider the things of old.
    Behold, I will do a new thing,
    Now it shall spring forth;
    Shall you not know it?
    I will even make a road in the wilderness
    And rivers in the desert."

ISAIAH 43:18–19

Children's children are the crown of old men,
    And the glory of children is their father.

PROVERBS 17:6

Behold, children are a heritage from the Lord,
   The fruit of the womb is a reward.
   Like arrows in the hand of a warrior,
   So are the children of one's youth.
   Happy is the man who has his quiver full of
      them;
   They shall not be ashamed,
   But shall speak with their enemies in the gate.

Psalm 127:3–5

You Forgive Your Children When They've Done Wrong

Blessed is he whose transgression is forgiven,
    Whose sin is covered.
    Blessed is the man to whom the LORD does not
        impute iniquity,
    And in whose spirit there is no deceit. . . .
    I acknowledged my sin to You,
    And my iniquity I have not hidden.
    I said, "I will confess my transgressions to the
        LORD,"
    And You forgave the iniquity of my sin.

PSALM 32:1–2, 5

He made known His ways to Moses,
    His acts to the children of Israel.
    The LORD is merciful and gracious,
    Slow to anger, and abounding in mercy.
    He will not always strive with us,
    Nor will He keep His anger forever.
    He has not dealt with us according to our sins,
    Nor punished us according to our iniquities.
    For as the heavens are high above the earth,
    So great is His mercy toward those who fear Him;
    As far as the east is from the west,
    So far has He removed our transgressions
        from us.
    As a father pities his children,
    So the LORD pities those who fear Him.

PSALM 103:7–13

"Take heed to yourselves. If your brother sins against you, rebuke him; and if he repents, forgive him. And if he sins against you seven times in a day, and seven times in a day returns to you, saying, 'I repent,' you shall forgive him."

LUKE 17:3–4

And you, being dead in your trespasses and the uncircumcision of your flesh, He has made alive together with Him, having forgiven you all trespasses, having wiped out the handwriting of requirements that was against us, which was contrary to us. And He has taken it out of the way, having nailed it to the cross. Having disarmed principalities and powers, He made a public spectacle of them, triumphing over them in it.

COLOSSIANS 2:13–15

Confess your trespasses to one another, and pray for one another, that you may be healed. The effective, fervent prayer of a righteous man avails much. Elijah was a man with a nature like ours, and he prayed earnestly that it would not rain; and it did not rain on the land for three years and six months.

JAMES 5:16–17

For You, Lord, are good, and ready to forgive,
    And abundant in mercy to all those who call
        upon You.
    Give ear, O Lord, to my prayer;
    And attend to the voice of my supplications.
    In the day of my trouble I will call upon You,
    For You will answer me.

Psalm 86:5–7

"Judge not, and you shall not be judged. Condemn not, and you shall not be condemned. Forgive, and you will be forgiven. Give, and it will be given to you: good measure, pressed down, shaken together, and running over will be put into your bosom. For with the same measure that you use, it will be measured back to you."

Luke 6:37–38

You Bring Your Family Together to Pray

The LORD is near to all who call upon Him,
>   To all who call upon Him in truth.
>   He will fulfill the desire of those who fear Him;
>   He also will hear their cry and save them.

PSALM 145:18–19

"Again I say to you that if two of you agree on earth concerning anything that they ask, it will be done for them by My Father in heaven. For where two or three are gathered together in My name, I am there in the midst of them."

MATTHEW 18:19–20

"Call to Me, and I will answer you, and show you great and mighty things, which you do not know."

JEREMIAH 33:3

Then I set my face toward the Lord God to make request by prayer and supplications, with fasting, sackcloth, and ashes. And I prayed to the LORD my God, and made confession, and said, "O Lord, great and awesome God, who keeps His covenant and mercy with those who love Him, and with those who keep His commandments, we have sinned and committed iniquity, we have done wickedly and rebelled, even by departing from Your precepts and Your judgments. . . .

"Now therefore, our God, hear the prayer of Your servant, and his supplications, and for the Lord's sake cause Your face to shine on Your sanctuary, which is desolate. O my God, incline Your ear and hear; open Your eyes and see our desolations, and the city which is called by Your name; for we do not present our supplications before You because of our righteous deeds, but because of Your great mercies."

DANIEL 9:3–5, 17–18

I desire therefore that the men pray everywhere, lifting up holy hands, without wrath and doubting.

1 TIMOTHY 2:8

Seeing then that we have a great High Priest who has passed through the heavens, Jesus the Son of God, let us hold fast our confession. For we do not have a High Priest who cannot sympathize with our weaknesses, but was in all points tempted as we are, yet without sin. Let us therefore come boldly to the throne of grace, that we may obtain mercy and find grace to help in time of need.

HEBREWS 4:14–16

My little children, let us not love in word or in tongue, but in deed and in truth. . . . For if our heart condemns us, God is greater than our heart, and knows all things. Beloved, if our heart does not condemn us, we have confidence toward God. And whatever we ask we receive from Him, because we keep His commandments and do those things that are pleasing in His sight.

1 JOHN 3:18, 20–22

You Share Your Family's Blessings with the Poor

He who has a generous eye will be blessed,
For he gives of his bread to the poor.

PROVERBS 22:9

He who oppresses the poor reproaches his Maker,
But he who honors Him has mercy on the needy.

PROVERBS 14:31

Listen, my beloved brethren: Has God not chosen the poor of this world to be rich in faith and heirs of the kingdom which He promised to those who love Him?

JAMES 2:5

What does it profit, my brethren, if someone says he has faith but does not have works? Can faith save him? If a brother or sister is naked and destitute of daily food, and one of you says to them, "Depart in peace, be warmed and filled," but you do not give them the things which are needed for the body, what does it profit? Thus also faith by itself, if it does not have works, is dead.

James 2:14–17

The Lord makes poor and makes rich;
> He brings low and lifts up.
> He raises the poor from the dust
> And lifts the beggar from the ash heap,
> To set them among princes
> And make them inherit the throne of glory.
> "For the pillars of the earth are the Lord's,
> And He has set the world upon them."

1 Samuel 2:7–8

You shall surely give to him, and your heart should not be grieved when you give to him, because for this thing the LORD your God will bless you in all your works and in all to which you put your hand. For the poor will never cease from the land; therefore I command you, saying, "You shall open your hand wide to your brother, to your poor and your needy, in your land."

DEUTERONOMY 15:10–11

Jesus said to him, "If you want to be perfect, go, sell what you have and give to the poor, and you will have treasure in heaven; and come, follow Me."

But when the young man heard that saying, he went away sorrowful, for he had great possessions.

Then Jesus said to His disciples, "Assuredly, I say to you that it is hard for a rich man to enter the kingdom of heaven. And again I say to you, it is easier for a camel to go through the eye of a needle than for a rich man to enter the kingdom of God."

MATTHEW 19:21–24

You Dedicate Your Children to the Lord

And now, little children, abide in Him, that when He appears, we may have confidence and not be ashamed before Him at His coming. If you know that He is righteous, you know that everyone who practices righteousness is born of Him.

1 JOHN 2:28–29

But now, O LORD,
  You are our Father;
  We are the clay, and You our potter;
  And all we are the work of Your hand.

ISAIAH 64:8

The righteous man walks in his integrity;
  His children are blessed after him.

PROVERBS 20:7

"The sun shall no longer be your light by day,
    Nor for brightness shall the moon give light
       to you;
    But the Lord will be to you an everlasting light,
    And your God your glory.
    Your sun shall no longer go down,
    Nor shall your moon withdraw itself;
    For the Lord will be your everlasting light,
    And the days of your mourning shall be ended.
    Also your people shall all be righteous;
    They shall inherit the land forever,
    The branch of My planting,
    The work of My hands,
    That I may be glorified.
    A little one shall become a thousand,
    And a small one a strong nation.
    I, the Lord, will hasten it in its time."

Isaiah 60:19–22

For as many of you as were baptized into Christ have put on Christ. There is neither Jew nor Greek, there is neither slave nor free, there is neither male nor female; for you are all one in Christ Jesus.

Galatians 3:27–28

"Their descendants shall be known among the
    Gentiles,
And their offspring among the people.
All who see them shall acknowledge them,
That they are the posterity whom the Lord
    has blessed."
I will greatly rejoice in the Lord,
My soul shall be joyful in my God;
For He has clothed me with the garments of
    salvation,
He has covered me with the robe of
    righteousness,
As a bridegroom decks himself with ornaments,
And as a bride adorns herself with her jewels.
For as the earth brings forth its bud,
As the garden causes the things that are sown in
    it to spring forth,
So the Lord God will cause righteousness and
    praise to spring forth before all the nations.

Isaiah 61:9–11

Children's children are the crown of old men,
 And the glory of children is their father.

PROVERBS 17:6

The LORD takes pleasure in those who fear Him,
 In those who hope in His mercy. . . .
 For He has strengthened the bars of your gates;
 He has blessed your children within you.
 He makes peace in your borders,
 And fills you with the finest wheat.

PSALM 147:11, 13–14

"Yet hear now, O Jacob My servant,
And Israel whom I have chosen.
Thus says the LORD who made you
And formed you from the womb, who will help you:
'Fear not, O Jacob My servant;
And you, Jeshurun, whom I have chosen.
For I will pour water on him who is thirsty,
And floods on the dry ground;
I will pour My Spirit on your descendants,
And My blessing on your offspring.'"

ISAIAH 44:1–3

GOD
ENCOURAGES
YOU TO . . .

Teach Your Children the Love of God

⁕

He came to His own, and His own did not receive Him. But as many as received Him, to them He gave the right to become children of God, to those who believe in His name.

JOHN 1:11–12

Yet in all these things we are more than conquerors through Him who loved us. For I am persuaded that neither death nor life, nor angels nor principalities nor powers, nor things present nor things to come, nor height nor depth, nor any other created thing, shall be able to separate us from the love of God which is in Christ Jesus our Lord.

ROMANS 8:37–39

I write to you, little children,
>Because your sins are forgiven you for His
>>name's sake.

I write to you, fathers,
>Because you have known Him who is
>>from the beginning.

I write to you, young men,
>Because you have overcome the wicked one.

I write to you, little children,
>Because you have known the Father.

I have written to you, fathers,
>Because you have known Him who is
>>from the beginning.

I have written to you, young men,
>Because you are strong, and the word of God
>>abides in you,
>And you have overcome the wicked one.

Do not love the world or the things in the world. If anyone loves the world, the love of the Father is not in him. For all that is in the world—the lust of the flesh, the lust of the eyes, and the pride of life—is not of the Father but is of the world. And the world is passing away, and the lust of it; but he who does the will of God abides forever.

1 John 2:12–17

Beloved, let us love one another, for love is of God; and everyone who loves is born of God and knows God. He who does not love does not know God, for God is love. In this the love of God was manifested toward us, that God has sent His only begotten Son into the world, that we might live through Him. In this is love, not that we loved God, but that He loved us and sent His Son to be the propitiation for our sins. Beloved, if God so loved us, we also ought to love one another.

No one has seen God at any time. If we love one another, God abides in us, and His love has been perfected in us. By this we know that we abide in Him, and He in us, because He has given us of His Spirit. And we have seen and testify that the Father has sent the Son as Savior of the world. Whoever confesses that Jesus is the Son of God, God abides in him, and he in God. And we have known and believed the love that God has for us. God is love, and he who abides in love abides in God, and God in him.

Love has been perfected among us in this: that we may have boldness in the day of judgment; because as He is, so are we in this world. There is no fear in love; but perfect love casts out fear, because fear involves torment. But he who fears has not been made perfect in love. We love Him because He first loved us.

If someone says, "I love God," and hates his brother, he is a liar; for he who does not love his brother whom he has seen, how can he love God whom he has not seen? And this commandment we have from Him: that he who loves God must love his brother also.

1 John 4:7–21

Then little children were brought to Him that He might put His hands on them and pray, but the disciples rebuked them. But Jesus said, "Let the little children come to Me, and do not forbid them; for of such is the kingdom of heaven." And He laid His hands on them and departed from there.

Matthew 19:13–15

For this is the love of God, that we keep His commandments. And His commandments are not burdensome. For whatever is born of God overcomes the world. And this is the victory that has overcome the world—our faith. Who is he who overcomes the world, but he who believes that Jesus is the Son of God?

1 JOHN 5:3–5

Christ may dwell in your hearts through faith; that you, being rooted and grounded in love, may be able to comprehend with all the saints what is the width and length and depth and height—to know the love of Christ which passes knowledge; that you may be filled with all the fullness of God.

EPHESIANS 3:17–19

Grow in Your Own Christian Walk

---*---

Teach me, O Lord, the way of Your statutes,
    And I shall keep it to the end.
    Give me understanding, and I shall keep
        Your law;
    Indeed, I shall observe it with my whole heart.
    Make me walk in the path of Your commandments,
    For I delight in it.
    Incline my heart to Your testimonies,
    And not to covetousness.
    Turn away my eyes from looking at worthless
        things,
    And revive me in Your way.
    Establish Your word to Your servant,
    Who is devoted to fearing You.

Psalm 119:33–38

Now by this we know that we know Him, if we keep His commandments. He who says, "I know Him," and does not keep His commandments, is a liar, and the truth is not in him. But whoever keeps His word, truly the love of God is perfected in him. By this we know that we are in Him. He who says he abides in Him ought himself also to walk just as He walked.

1 John 2:3–6

Teach me Your way, O Lord;
    I will walk in Your truth;
    Unite my heart to fear Your name.
    I will praise You, O Lord my God, with all
        my heart,
    And I will glorify Your name forevermore.

Psalm 86:11–12

Show me Your ways, O Lord;
    Teach me Your paths.
    Lead me in Your truth and teach me,
    For You are the God of my salvation;
    On You I wait all the day.

Psalm 25:4–5

And do this, knowing the time, that now it is high time to awake out of sleep; for now our salvation is nearer than when we first believed. The night is far spent, the day is at hand. Therefore let us cast off the works of darkness, and let us put on the armor of light. Let us walk properly, as in the day, not in revelry and drunkenness, not in lewdness and lust, not in strife and envy. But put on the Lord Jesus Christ, and make no provision for the flesh, to fulfill its lusts.

ROMANS 13:11–14

Your word is a lamp to my feet
    And a light to my path.
    I have sworn and confirmed
    That I will keep Your righteous judgments.
    I am afflicted very much;
    Revive me, O LORD, according to Your word.
    Accept, I pray, the freewill offerings of my
        mouth, O LORD,
    And teach me Your judgments.
    My life is continually in my hand,
    Yet I do not forget Your law.

PSALM 119:105–109

Whoever believes that Jesus is the Christ is born of God, and everyone who loves Him who begot also loves him who is begotten of Him. By this we know that we love the children of God, when we love God and keep His commandments. For this is the love of God, that we keep His commandments. And His commandments are not burdensome.

1 John 5:1–3

Therefore, having these promises, beloved, let us cleanse ourselves from all filthiness of the flesh and spirit, perfecting holiness in the fear of God.

2 Corinthians 7:1

How can a young man cleanse his way?
>By taking heed according to Your word.
>With my whole heart I have sought You;
>Oh, let me not wander from Your commandments!
>Your word I have hidden in my heart,
>That I might not sin against You.
>Blessed are You, O Lord!
>Teach me Your statutes.

Psalm 119:9–12

Share Your Faith with Your Children

───────── ✤ ─────────

But what does it say? "The word is near you, in your mouth and in your heart" (that is, the word of faith which we preach): that if you confess with your mouth the Lord Jesus and believe in your heart that God has raised Him from the dead, you will be saved. For with the heart one believes unto righteousness, and with the mouth confession is made unto salvation. For the Scripture says, "Whoever believes on Him will not be put to shame."

ROMANS 10:8–11

For this is good and acceptable in the sight of God our Savior, who desires all men to be saved and to come to the knowledge of the truth.

1 TIMOTHY 2:3–4

Then Jesus called a little child to Him, set him in the midst of them, and said, "Assuredly, I say to you, unless you are converted and become as little children, you will by no means enter the kingdom of heaven. Therefore whoever humbles himself as this little child is the greatest in the kingdom of heaven. Whoever receives one little child like this in My name receives Me.

"Whoever causes one of these little ones who believe in Me to sin, it would be better for him if a millstone were hung around his neck, and he were drowned in the depth of the sea. . . .

"Take heed that you do not despise one of these little ones, for I say to you that in heaven their angels always see the face of My Father who is in heaven. For the Son of Man has come to save that which was lost.

"What do you think? If a man has a hundred sheep, and one of them goes astray, does he not leave the ninety-nine and go to the mountains to seek the one that is straying? And if he should find it, assuredly, I say to you, he rejoices more over that sheep than over the ninety-nine that did not go astray. Even so it is not the will of your Father who is in heaven that one of these little ones should perish."

MATTHEW 18:2–6, 10–14

"And these words which I command you today shall be in your heart. You shall teach them diligently to your children, and shall talk of them when you sit in your house, when you walk by the way, when you lie down, and when you rise up. You shall bind them as a sign on your hand, and they shall be as frontlets between your eyes. You shall write them on the door-posts of your house and on your gates."

DEUTERONOMY 6:6–9

But before faith came, we were kept under guard by the law, kept for the faith which would afterward be revealed. Therefore the law was our tutor to bring us to Christ, that we might be justified by faith. But after faith has come, we are no longer under a tutor.

For you are all sons of God through faith in Christ Jesus. For as many of you as were baptized into Christ have put on Christ.

GALATIANS 3:23–27

For the equipping of the saints for the work of ministry, for the edifying of the body of Christ, till we all come to the unity of the faith and of the knowledge of the Son of God, to a perfect man, to the measure of the stature of the fullness of Christ; that we should no longer be children, tossed to and fro and carried about with every wind of doctrine, by the trickery of men, in the cunning craftiness of deceitful plotting, but, speaking the truth in love, may grow up in all things into Him who is the head—Christ.

EPHESIANS 4:12–15

Then they brought little children to Him, that He might touch them; but the disciples rebuked those who brought them. But when Jesus saw it, He was greatly displeased and said to them, "Let the little children come to Me, and do not forbid them; for of such is the kingdom of God. Assuredly, I say to you, whoever does not receive the kingdom of God as a little child will by no means enter it." And He took them up in His arms, laid His hands on them, and blessed them.

MARK 10:13–16

So then faith comes by hearing, and hearing by the word of God.

Romans 10:17

For the love of Christ compels us, because we judge thus: that if One died for all, then all died; and He died for all, that those who live should live no longer for themselves, but for Him who died for them and rose again.

Therefore, from now on, we regard no one according to the flesh. Even though we have known Christ according to the flesh, yet now we know Him thus no longer. Therefore, if anyone is in Christ, he is a new creation; old things have passed away; behold, all things have become new.

2 Corinthians 5:14–17

Deal Honestly with Those Close to You

———— ❖ ————

Lying lips are an abomination to the LORD,
But those who deal truthfully are His delight.

PROVERBS 12:22

"Judge not, that you be not judged. For with what judgment you judge, you will be judged; and with the measure you use, it will be measured back to you. And why do you look at the speck in your brother's eye, but do not consider the plank in your own eye? Or how can you say to your brother, 'Let me remove the speck from your eye'; and look, a plank is in your own eye? Hypocrite! First remove the plank from your own eye, and then you will see clearly to remove the speck from your brother's eye."

MATTHEW 7:1–5

Let Your mercies come also to me, O LORD—
Your salvation according to Your word.
So shall I have an answer for him who
reproaches me,
For I trust in Your word.
And take not the word of truth utterly out of
my mouth,
For I have hoped in Your ordinances.
So shall I keep Your law continually,
Forever and ever.
And I will walk at liberty,
For I seek Your precepts.
I will speak of Your testimonies also before
kings,
And will not be ashamed.
And I will delight myself in Your commandments,
Which I love.
My hands also I will lift up to Your
commandments,
Which I love,
And I will meditate on Your statutes.

PSALM 119:41–48

If indeed you have heard Him and have been taught by Him, as the truth is in Jesus: that you put off, concerning your former conduct, the old man which grows corrupt according to the deceitful lusts, and be renewed in the spirit of your mind, and that you put on the new man which was created according to God, in true righteousness and holiness.

Therefore, putting away lying, "Let each one of you speak truth with his neighbor," for we are members of one another. . . . Let no corrupt word proceed out of your mouth, but what is good for necessary edification, that it may impart grace to the hearers. And do not grieve the Holy Spirit of God, by whom you were sealed for the day of redemption.

Ephesians 4:21–25, 29–30

Do not lie to one another, since you have put off the old man with his deeds, and have put on the new man who is renewed in knowledge according to the image of Him who created him.

Colossians 3:9–10

Do not withhold good from those to whom it is due,
When it is in the power of your hand to do so.

PROVERBS 3:27

He who is often rebuked, and hardens his neck,
Will suddenly be destroyed, and that without
remedy.

PROVERBS 29:1

Never Stop Loving Your Wife

⁂

Live joyfully with the wife whom you love all the days of your vain life which He has given you under the sun, all your days of vanity; for that is your portion in life, and in the labor which you perform under the sun.

ECCLESIASTES 9:9

He who finds a wife finds a good thing,
    And obtains favor from the LORD.

PROVERBS 18:22

Let your fountain be blessed,
    And rejoice with the wife of your youth.
    As a loving deer and a graceful doe,
    Let her breasts satisfy you at all times;
    And always be enraptured with her love.

PROVERBS 5:18–19

And He answered and said to them, "Have you not read that He who made them at the beginning 'made them male and female,' and said, 'For this reason a man shall leave his father and mother and be joined to his wife, and the two shall become one flesh'? So then, they are no longer two but one flesh. Therefore what God has joined together, let not man separate."

Matthew 19:4–6

And the Lord God said, "It is not good that man should be alone; I will make him a helper comparable to him."

Genesis 2:18

"But from the beginning of the creation, God 'made them male and female.' 'For this reason a man shall leave his father and mother and be joined to his wife, and the two shall become one flesh'; so then they are no longer two, but one flesh. Therefore what God has joined together, let not man separate."

Mark 10:6–9

How fair is your love,
    My sister, my spouse!
    How much better than wine is your love,
    And the scent of your perfumes
    Than all spices!
    Your lips, O my spouse,
    Drip as the honeycomb;
    Honey and milk are under your tongue;
    And the fragrance of your garments
    Is like the fragrance of Lebanon.
    A garden enclosed
    Is my sister, my spouse,
    A spring shut up,
    A fountain sealed.
    Your plants are an orchard of pomegranates
    With pleasant fruits,
    Fragrant henna with spikenard,
    Spikenard and saffron,
    Calamus and cinnamon,
    With all trees of frankincense,
    Myrrh and aloes,
    With all the chief spices—
    A fountain of gardens,

A well of living waters,
And streams from Lebanon.
Awake, O north wind,
And come, O south!
Blow upon my garden,
That its spices may flow out.
Let my beloved come to his garden
And eat its pleasant fruits.

Song of Solomon 4:10–16

Nevertheless, because of sexual immorality, let each man have his own wife, and let each woman have her own husband. Let the husband render to his wife the affection due her, and likewise also the wife to her husband. The wife does not have authority over her own body, but the husband does. And likewise the husband does not have authority over his own body, but the wife does. Do not deprive one another except with consent for a time, that you may give yourselves to fasting and prayer; and come together again so that Satan does not tempt you because of your lack of self-control. But I say this as a concession, not as a commandment.

1 Corinthians 7:2–6

Houses and riches are an inheritance from fathers,
But a prudent wife is from the LORD.

PROVERBS 19:14

Marriage is honorable among all, and the bed undefiled; but fornicators and adulterers God will judge.

HEBREWS 13:4

Be Wise with Your Family Finances

———— ✦ ————

"Bring all the tithes into the storehouse,
    That there may be food in My house,
    And try Me now in this,"
    Says the Lord of hosts,
    "If I will not open for you the windows of
        heaven
    And pour out for you such blessing
    That there will not be room enough to receive it."

MALACHI 3:10

"And you shall remember the Lord your God, for it is He who gives you power to get wealth, that He may establish His covenant which He swore to your fathers, as it is this day."

DEUTERONOMY 8:18

The LORD makes poor and makes rich;
> He brings low and lifts up.
> He raises the poor from the dust
> And lifts the beggar from the ash heap,
> To set them among princes
> And make them inherit the throne of glory.
> "For the pillars of the earth are the LORD's,
> And He has set the world upon them.
> He will guard the feet of His saints,
> But the wicked shall be silent in darkness.
> "For by strength no man shall prevail.

1 SAMUEL 2:7–9

"So that you do not appear to men to be fasting, but to your Father who is in the secret place; and your Father who sees in secret will reward you openly.

"Do not lay up for yourselves treasures on earth, where moth and rust destroy and where thieves break in and steal; but lay up for yourselves treasures in heaven, where neither moth nor rust destroys and where thieves do not break in and steal. For where your treasure is, there your heart will be also."

MATTHEW 6:18–21

But if anyone does not provide for his own, and especially for those of his household, he has denied the faith and is worse than an unbeliever.

1 TIMOTHY 5:8

Now it shall come to pass, if you diligently obey the voice of the LORD your God, to observe carefully all His commandments which I command you today, that the LORD your God will set you high above all nations of the earth. And all these blessings shall come upon you and overtake you, because you obey the voice of the LORD your God:

Blessed shall you be in the city, and blessed shall you be in the country.

Blessed shall be the fruit of your body, the produce of your ground and the increase of your herds, the increase of your cattle and the offspring of your flocks.

Blessed shall be your basket and your kneading bowl.

Blessed shall you be when you come in, and blessed shall you be when you go out.

DEUTERONOMY 28:1–6

Through wisdom a house is built,
   And by understanding it is established;
   By knowledge the rooms are filled
   With all precious and pleasant riches.
   A wise man is strong,
   Yes, a man of knowledge increases strength;
   For by wise counsel you will wage your own war,
   And in a multitude of counselors there is safety.

Proverbs 24:3–6

Better is a little with righteousness,
   Than vast revenues without justice.

Proverbs 16:8

Now godliness with contentment is great gain. For we brought nothing into this world, and it is certain we can carry nothing out. And having food and clothing, with these we shall be content. But those who desire to be rich fall into temptation and a snare, and into many foolish and harmful lusts which drown men in destruction and perdition. For the love of money is a root of all kinds of evil, for which some have strayed from the faith in their greediness, and pierced themselves through with many sorrows.

1 TIMOTHY 6:6–10

Bring Your Tithe to the Storehouse

———— ❖ ————

Honor the LORD with your possessions,
    And with the firstfruits of all your increase;
    So your barns will be filled with plenty,
    And your vats will overflow with new wine.

PROVERBS 3:9–10

Three times a year all your males shall appear before the LORD your God in the place which He chooses: at the Feast of Unleavened Bread, at the Feast of Weeks, and at the Feast of Tabernacles; and they shall not appear before the LORD empty-handed. Every man shall give as he is able, according to the blessing of the LORD your God which He has given you.

DEUTERONOMY 16:16–17

"Give, and it will be given to you: good measure, pressed down, shaken together, and running over will be put into your bosom. For with the same measure that you use, it will be measured back to you."

LUKE 6:38

Give to the LORD, O families of the peoples,
    Give to the LORD glory and strength.
    Give to the LORD the glory due His name;
    Bring an offering, and come into His courts.
    Oh, worship the LORD in the beauty of holiness!
    Tremble before Him, all the earth.

PSALM 96:7–9

Now concerning the collection for the saints, as I have given orders to the churches of Galatia, so you must do also: On the first day of the week let each one of you lay something aside, storing up as he may prosper, that there be no collections when I come.

1 CORINTHIANS 16:1–2

But this I say: He who sows sparingly will also reap sparingly, and he who sows bountifully will also reap bountifully. So let each one give as he purposes in his heart, not grudgingly or of necessity; for God loves a cheerful giver. And God is able to make all grace abound toward you, that you, always having all sufficiency in all things, may have an abundance for every good work. As it is written:

"He has dispersed abroad,
He has given to the poor;
His righteousness endures forever."

Now may He who supplies seed to the sower, and bread for food, supply and multiply the seed you have sown and increase the fruits of your righteousness, while you are enriched in everything for all liberality, which causes thanksgiving through us to God. For the administration of this service not only supplies the needs of the saints, but also is abounding through many thanksgivings to God.

2 Corinthians 9:6–12

"Will a man rob God?
　　Yet you have robbed Me!
　　But you say,
　　'In what way have we robbed You?'
　　In tithes and offerings.
　　You are cursed with a curse,
　　For you have robbed Me,
　　Even this whole nation.
　　Bring all the tithes into the storehouse,
　　That there may be food in My house,
　　And try Me now in this,"
　　Says the LORD of hosts,
　　"If I will not open for you the windows of heaven
　　And pour out for you such blessing
　　That there will not be room enough to receive it.
　　And I will rebuke the devourer for your sakes,
　　So that he will not destroy the fruit of your ground,
　　Nor shall the vine fail to bear fruit for you in
　　　　the field,"
　　Says the LORD of hosts;
　　"And all nations will call you blessed,
　　For you will be a delightful land,"
　　Says the LORD of hosts.

MALACHI 3:8–12

The righteous shall flourish like a palm tree,
  He shall grow like a cedar in Lebanon.
  Those who are planted in the house of the LORD
  Shall flourish in the courts of our God.
  They shall still bear fruit in old age;
  They shall be fresh and flourishing,
  To declare that the LORD is upright;
  He is my rock, and there is no
    unrighteousness in Him.

PSALM 92:12–15

GOD
COMFORTS
YOU WHEN . . .

You Feel Inadequate in Raising Your Children

———— ❖ ————

By which have been given to us exceedingly great and precious promises, that through these you may be partakers of the divine nature, having escaped the corruption that is in the world through lust.

But also for this very reason, giving all diligence, add to your faith virtue, to virtue knowledge, to knowledge self-control, to self-control perseverance, to perseverance godliness, to godliness brotherly kindness, and to brotherly kindness love. For if these things are yours and abound, you will be neither barren nor unfruitful in the knowledge of our Lord Jesus Christ.

2 PETER 1:4–8

"The Lord GOD has given Me
    The tongue of the learned,
    That I should know how to speak
    A word in season to him who is weary.
    He awakens Me morning by morning,
    He awakens My ear
    To hear as the learned.
    The Lord GOD has opened My ear;
    And I was not rebellious,
    Nor did I turn away.
    I gave My back to those who struck Me,
    And My cheeks to those who plucked out the
        beard;
    I did not hide My face from shame and spitting.
    For the Lord GOD will help Me;
    Therefore I will not be disgraced;
    Therefore I have set My face like a flint,
    And I know that I will not be ashamed."

ISAIAH 50:4–7

LORD, my heart is not haughty,
    Nor my eyes lofty.
    Neither do I concern myself with great matters,
    Nor with things too profound for me.
    Surely I have calmed and quieted my soul,
    Like a weaned child with his mother;
    Like a weaned child is my soul within me.
    O Israel, hope in the LORD
    From this time forth and forever.

PSALM 131:1–3

"Remember these, O Jacob,
    And Israel, for you are My servant;
    I have formed you, you are My servant;
    O Israel, you will not be forgotten by Me!
    I have blotted out, like a thick cloud, your
        transgressions,
    And like a cloud, your sins.
    Return to Me, for I have redeemed you."

ISAIAH 44:21–22

But the Lord stood with me and strengthened me, so that the message might be preached fully through me, and that all the Gentiles might hear. Also I was delivered out of the mouth of the lion. And the Lord will deliver me from every evil work and preserve me for His heavenly kingdom. To Him be glory forever and ever. Amen!

2 TIMOTHY 4:17–18

"Come to Me, all you who labor and are heavy laden, and I will give you rest. Take My yoke upon you and learn from Me, for I am gentle and lowly in heart, and you will find rest for your souls. For My yoke is easy and My burden is light."

MATTHEW 11:28–30

"But You are the same,
    And Your years will have no end.
    The children of Your servants will continue,
    And their descendants will be established
        before You."

PSALM 102:27–28

Not that I speak in regard to need, for I have learned in whatever state I am, to be content: I know how to be abased, and I know how to abound. Everywhere and in all things I have learned both to be full and to be hungry, both to abound and to suffer need. I can do all things through Christ who strengthens me.

Philippians 4:11–13

And we have such trust through Christ toward God. Not that we are sufficient of ourselves to think of anything as being from ourselves, but our sufficiency is from God, who also made us sufficient as ministers of the new covenant, not of the letter but of the Spirit; for the letter kills, but the Spirit gives life.

2 Corinthians 3:4–6

Your Child Is Seriously Ill

When Jesus came into the ruler's house, and saw the flute players and the noisy crowd wailing, He said to them, "Make room, for the girl is not dead, but sleeping." And they ridiculed Him. But when the crowd was put outside, He went in and took her by the hand, and the girl arose. And the report of this went out into all that land.

MATTHEW 9:23–26

"As one whom his mother comforts,
So I will comfort you;
And you shall be comforted in Jerusalem."

ISAIAH 66:13

Beloved, I pray that you may prosper in all things and be in health, just as your soul prospers.

3 JOHN 2

Then one of the crowd answered and said, "Teacher, I brought You my son, who has a mute spirit. And wherever it seizes him, it throws him down; he foams at the mouth, gnashes his teeth, and becomes rigid. So I spoke to Your disciples, that they should cast it out, but they could not."

He answered him and said, "O faithless generation, how long shall I be with you? How long shall I bear with you? Bring him to Me." Then they brought him to Him. And when he saw Him, immediately the spirit convulsed him, and he fell on the ground and wallowed, foaming at the mouth.

So He asked his father, "How long has this been happening to him?"

And he said, "From childhood. And often he has thrown him both into the fire and into the water to destroy him. But if You can do anything, have compassion on us and help us."

Jesus said to him, "If you can believe, all things are possible to him who believes."

Immediately the father of the child cried out and said with tears, "Lord, I believe; help my unbelief!"

MARK 9:17–24

Now when Jesus had entered Capernaum, a centurion came to Him, pleading with Him, saying, "Lord, my servant is lying at home paralyzed, dreadfully tormented."

And Jesus said to him, "I will come and heal him."

The centurion answered and said, "Lord, I am not worthy that You should come under my roof. But only speak a word, and my servant will be healed. For I also am a man under authority, having soldiers under me. And I say to this one, 'Go,' and he goes; and to another, 'Come,' and he comes; and to my servant, 'Do this,' and he does it."

When Jesus heard it, He marveled, and said to those who followed, "Assuredly, I say to you, I have not found such great faith, not even in Israel! And I say to you that many will come from east and west, and sit down with Abraham, Isaac, and Jacob in the kingdom of heaven. But the sons of the kingdom will be cast out into outer darkness. There will be weeping and gnashing of teeth." Then Jesus said to the centurion, "Go your way; and as you have believed, so let it be done for you." And his servant was healed that same hour.

MATTHEW 8:5–13

Is anyone among you sick? Let him call for the elders of the church, and let them pray over him, anointing him with oil in the name of the Lord. And the prayer of faith will save the sick, and the Lord will raise him up. And if he has committed sins, he will be forgiven. Confess your trespasses to one another, and pray for one another, that you may be healed. The effective, fervent prayer of a righteous man avails much.

JAMES 5:14–16

Your Wife Doesn't Seem to Understand

———— ✛ ————

Two are better than one,
>   Because they have a good reward for their labor.
>   For if they fall, one will lift up his companion.
>   But woe to him who is alone when he falls,
>   For he has no one to help him up.
>   Again, if two lie down together, they will keep
>   warm;
>   But how can one be warm alone?

ECCLESIASTES 4:9–11

A word fitly spoken is like apples of gold
>   In settings of silver. . . .
>   By long forbearance a ruler is persuaded,
>   And a gentle tongue breaks a bone.

PROVERBS 25:11, 15

Husbands, likewise, dwell with them with understanding, giving honor to the wife, as to the weaker vessel, and as being heirs together of the grace of life, that your prayers may not be hindered.

Finally, all of you be of one mind, having compassion for one another; love as brothers, be tenderhearted, be courteous; not returning evil for evil or reviling for reviling, but on the contrary blessing, knowing that you were called to this, that you may inherit a blessing. For

"He who would love life
And see good days,
Let him refrain his tongue from evil,
And his lips from speaking deceit.
Let him turn away from evil and do good;
Let him seek peace and pursue it."

1 Peter 3:7–11

Though I speak with the tongues of men and of angels, but have not love, I have become sounding brass or a clanging cymbal. And though I have the gift of prophecy, and understand all mysteries and all knowledge, and though I have all faith, so that

I could remove mountains, but have not love, I am nothing. And though I bestow all my goods to feed the poor, and though I give my body to be burned, but have not love, it profits me nothing.

Love suffers long and is kind; love does not envy; love does not parade itself, is not puffed up; does not behave rudely, does not seek its own, is not provoked, thinks no evil; does not rejoice in iniquity, but rejoices in the truth; bears all things, believes all things, hopes all things, endures all things.

Love never fails. But whether there are prophecies, they will fail; whether there are tongues, they will cease; whether there is knowledge, it will vanish away. For we know in part and we prophesy in part. But when that which is perfect has come, then that which is in part will be done away.

When I was a child, I spoke as a child, I understood as a child, I thought as a child; but when I became a man, I put away childish things. For now we see in a mirror, dimly, but then face to face. Now I know in part, but then I shall know just as I also am known.

And now abide faith, hope, love, these three; but the greatest of these is love.

1 Corinthians 13:1–13

Let love be without hypocrisy. Abhor what is evil. Cling to what is good. Be kindly affectionate to one another with brotherly love, in honor giving preference to one another.

ROMANS 12:9–10

Nevertheless, neither is man independent of woman, nor woman independent of man, in the Lord. For as woman came from man, even so man also comes through woman; but all things are from God.

1 CORINTHIANS 11:11–12

Owe no one anything except to love one another, for he who loves another has fulfilled the law. For the commandments, "You shall not commit adultery," "You shall not murder," "You shall not steal," "You shall not bear false witness," "You shall not covet," and if there is any other commandment, are all summed up in this saying, namely, "You shall love your neighbor as yourself." Love does no harm to a neighbor; therefore love is the fulfillment of the law.

ROMANS 13:8–10

You Must Discipline
Your Children

My son, do not despise the chastening of the LORD,
    Nor detest His correction;
    For whom the LORD loves He corrects,
    Just as a father the son in whom he delights.

PROVERBS 3:11–12

The rod and rebuke give wisdom,
    But a child left to himself brings shame to his
        mother. . . .
    Correct your son, and he will give you rest;
    Yes, he will give delight to your soul.

PROVERBS 29:15, 17

Though He was a Son, yet He learned obedience by the things which He suffered.

HEBREWS 5:8

Chasten your son while there is hope,
    And do not set your heart on his destruction.

PROVERBS 19:18

Rebuke is more effective for a wise man
    Than a hundred blows on a fool.

PROVERBS 17:10

Furthermore, we have had human fathers who corrected us, and we paid them respect. Shall we not much more readily be in subjection to the Father of spirits and live? For they indeed for a few days chastened us as seemed best to them, but He for our profit, that we may be partakers of His holiness. Now no chastening seems to be joyful for the present, but painful; nevertheless, afterward it yields the peaceable fruit of righteousness to those who have been trained by it.

HEBREWS 12:9–11

Hatred stirs up strife,
>   But love covers all sins.
>   Wisdom is found on the lips of him who has
>   understanding,
>   But a rod is for the back of him who is devoid of
>   understanding.

PROVERBS 10:12–13

My son, keep my words,
>   And treasure my commands within you.
>   Keep my commands and live,
>   And my law as the apple of your eye.
>   Bind them on your fingers;
>   Write them on the tablet of your heart.

PROVERBS 7:1–3

Therefore be very courageous to keep and to do all that is written in the Book of the Law of Moses, lest you turn aside from it to the right hand or to the left. . . . But you shall hold fast to the LORD your God, as you have done to this day.

JOSHUA 23:6, 8

You Feel Powerless to Shield Your Children

※

"Come now, and let us reason together,"
>   Says the LORD,
>   "Though your sins are like scarlet,
>   They shall be as white as snow;
>   Though they are red like crimson,
>   They shall be as wool.
>   If you are willing and obedient,
>   You shall eat the good of the land;
>   But if you refuse and rebel,
>   You shall be devoured by the sword";
>   For the mouth of the LORD has spoken.

ISAIAH 1:18–20

In the fear of the LORD there is strong
       confidence,
   And His children will have a place of refuge.
   The fear of the LORD is a fountain of life,
   To turn one away from the snares of death.

PROVERBS 14:26–27

Therefore hear me now, my children,
   And do not depart from the words of my
       mouth. . . .
   Lest aliens be filled with your wealth,
   And your labors go to the house of a foreigner;
   And you mourn at last,
   When your flesh and your body are consumed,
   And say:
   "How I have hated instruction,
   And my heart despised correction!
   I have not obeyed the voice of my teachers,
   Nor inclined my ear to those who instructed
       me!
   I was on the verge of total ruin,
   In the midst of the assembly and congregation."

PROVERBS 5:7, 10–14

Wine is a mocker,
>Strong drink is a brawler,
>And whoever is led astray by it is not wise.

PROVERBS 20:1

In mercy and truth
>Atonement is provided for iniquity;
>And by the fear of the LORD one departs from evil.

PROVERBS 16:6

Do you not know that you are the temple of God and that the Spirit of God dwells in you? If anyone defiles the temple of God, God will destroy him. For the temple of God is holy, which temple you are.

1 CORINTHIANS 3:16–17

The merciful man does good for his own soul,
>But he who is cruel troubles his own flesh. . . .
>Though they join forces, the wicked will not go
>>unpunished;
>But the posterity of the righteous will be
>>delivered.

PROVERBS 11:17, 21

My son, if you receive my words,
    And treasure my commands within you,
    So that you incline your ear to wisdom,
    And apply your heart to understanding;
    Yes, if you cry out for discernment,
    And lift up your voice for understanding,
    If you seek her as silver,
    And search for her as for hidden treasures;
    Then you will understand the fear of the LORD,
    And find the knowledge of God.
    For the LORD gives wisdom;
    From His mouth come knowledge and
        understanding;
    He stores up sound wisdom for the upright;
    He is a shield to those who walk uprightly;
    He guards the paths of justice,
    And preserves the way of His saints.
    Then you will understand righteousness and
        justice,
    Equity and every good path.

PROVERBS 2:1–9

He who loves pleasure will be a poor man;
   He who loves wine and oil will not be rich.

PROVERBS 21:17

"And do not fear those who kill the body but cannot kill the soul. But rather fear Him who is able to destroy both soul and body in hell."

MATTHEW 10:28

GOD FILLS
YOU WITH JOY
WHEN . . .

Your Family Worships Together

———————— ❧ ————————

Now, behold, I have brought the firstfruits of the land which you, O LORD, have given me.

Then you shall set it before the LORD your God, and worship before the LORD your God. So you shall rejoice in every good thing which the LORD your God has given to you and your house, you and the Levite and the stranger who is among you.

DEUTERONOMY 26:10–11

Oh come, let us worship and bow down;
    Let us kneel before the LORD our Maker.
    For He is our God,
    And we are the people of His pasture,
    And the sheep of His hand.

PSALM 95:6–7

Exalt the LORD our God,
And worship at His holy hill;
For the LORD our God is holy.

PSALM 99:9

Make a joyful shout to the LORD, all you lands!
Serve the LORD with gladness;
Come before His presence with singing.
Know that the LORD, He is God;
It is He who has made us, and not we ourselves;
We are His people and the sheep of His pasture.

PSALM 100:1–3

Jesus said to her, "Woman, believe Me, the hour is coming when you will neither on this mountain, nor in Jerusalem, worship the Father. You worship what you do not know; we know what we worship, for salvation is of the Jews. But the hour is coming, and now is, when the true worshipers will worship the Father in spirit and truth; for the Father is seeking such to worship Him. God is Spirit, and those who worship Him must worship in spirit and truth."

JOHN 4:21–24

Then Jesus said to him, "Away with you, Satan! For it is written, 'You shall worship the LORD your God, and Him only you shall serve.'"

MATTHEW 4:10

Let the word of Christ dwell in you richly in all wisdom, teaching and admonishing one another in psalms and hymns and spiritual songs, singing with grace in your hearts to the Lord.

COLOSSIANS 3:16

The LORD lives!
    Blessed be my Rock!
    Let God be exalted,
    The Rock of my salvation!

2 SAMUEL 22:47

Your Children Grow to Love Him

I love those who love me,
And those who seek me diligently will find me.

PROVERBS 8:17

"You are the salt of the earth; but if the salt loses its flavor, how shall it be seasoned? It is then good for nothing but to be thrown out and trampled underfoot by men.

"You are the light of the world. A city that is set on a hill cannot be hidden. Nor do they light a lamp and put it under a basket, but on a lampstand, and it gives light to all who are in the house. Let your light so shine before men, that they may see your good works and glorify your Father in heaven."

MATTHEW 5:13–16

That Christ may dwell in your hearts through faith; that you, being rooted and grounded in love, may be able to comprehend with all the saints what is the width and length and depth and height—to know the love of Christ which passes knowledge; that you may be filled with all the fullness of God.

EPHESIANS 3:17–19

Grace to you and peace from God our Father and the Lord Jesus Christ.

I thank my God always concerning you for the grace of God which was given to you by Christ Jesus, that you were enriched in everything by Him in all utterance and all knowledge, even as the testimony of Christ was confirmed in you, so that you come short in no gift, eagerly waiting for the revelation of our Lord Jesus Christ, who will also confirm you to the end, that you may be blameless in the day of our Lord Jesus Christ. God is faithful, by whom you were called into the fellowship of His Son, Jesus Christ our Lord.

1 CORINTHIANS 1:3–9

We know that we all have knowledge. Knowledge puffs up, but love edifies. And if anyone thinks that he knows anything, he knows nothing yet as he ought to know. But if anyone loves God, this one is known by Him.

1 Corinthians 8:1–3

The Lord will establish you as a holy people to Himself, just as He has sworn to you, if you keep the commandments of the Lord your God and walk in His ways. Then all peoples of the earth shall see that you are called by the name of the Lord, and they shall be afraid of you.

Deuteronomy 28:9–10

Jesus said to him, "'You shall love the Lord your God with all your heart, with all your soul, and with all your mind.' This is the first and great commandment. And the second is like it: 'You shall love your neighbor as yourself.' On these two commandments hang all the Law and the Prophets."

Matthew 22:37–40

"'And you shall love the LORD your God with all your heart, with all your soul, with all your mind, and with all your strength.' This is the first commandment."

MARK 12:30

The LORD your God will bring you back from captivity, and have compassion on you, and gather you again from all the nations where the LORD your God has scattered you. If any of you are driven out to the farthest parts under heaven, from there the LORD your God will gather you, and from there He will bring you. Then the LORD your God will bring you to the land which your fathers possessed, and you shall possess it. He will prosper you and multiply you more than your fathers. And the LORD your God will circumcise your heart and the heart of your descendants, to love the LORD your God with all your heart and with all your soul, that you may live.

DEUTERONOMY 30:3–6

Your Family Gives
Praises to the Lord

I will extol You, my God, O King;
    And I will bless Your name forever and ever.
    Every day I will bless You,
    And I will praise Your name forever and ever.
    Great is the LORD, and greatly to be praised;
    And His greatness is unsearchable.
    One generation shall praise Your works to
        another,
    And shall declare Your mighty acts.

PSALM 145:1–4

This people I have formed for Myself;
    They shall declare My praise.

ISAIAH 43:21

Both young men and maidens;
　　Old men and children.
　　Let them praise the name of the LORD,
　　For His name alone is exalted;
　　His glory is above the earth and heaven.
　　And He has exalted the horn of His people,
　　The praise of all His saints—
　　Of the children of Israel,
　　A people near to Him.
　　Praise the LORD!

PSALM 148:12–14

Know that the LORD, He is God;
　　It is He who has made us, and not we ourselves;
　　We are His people and the sheep of His pasture.
　　Enter into His gates with thanksgiving,
　　And into His courts with praise.
　　Be thankful to Him, and bless His name.
　　For the LORD is good;
　　His mercy is everlasting,
　　And His truth endures to all generations.

PSALM 100:3–5

Praise the LORD!
 Praise God in His sanctuary;
 Praise Him in His mighty firmament!
 Praise Him for His mighty acts;
 Praise Him according to His excellent greatness!
 Praise Him with the sound of the trumpet;
 Praise Him with the lute and harp!
 Praise Him with the timbrel and dance;
 Praise Him with stringed instruments and flutes!
 Praise Him with loud cymbals;
 Praise Him with clashing cymbals!
 Let everything that has breath praise the LORD.
 Praise the LORD!

PSALM 150:1–6

I will call upon the LORD, who is worthy to be praised;
 So shall I be saved from my enemies.

2 SAMUEL 22:4

This will be written for the generation to come,
 That a people yet to be created may praise
  the LORD.

PSALM 102:18

I will sing of the mercies of the Lord forever;
> With my mouth will I make known Your
> > faithfulness to all generations.
> For I have said, "Mercy shall be built up forever;
> Your faithfulness You shall establish in the very
> > heavens."
> "I have made a covenant with My chosen,
> I have sworn to My servant David:
> 'Your seed I will establish forever,
> And build up your throne to all generations.'"

PSALM 89:1–4

I thank You and praise You,
> O God of my fathers;
> You have given me wisdom and might,
> And have now made known to me what we
> > asked of You,
> For You have made known to us the king's
> > demand.

DANIEL 2:23

Your Children Who Know His Love, Share It with Others

Therefore be imitators of God as dear children. And walk in love, as Christ also has loved us and given Himself for us, an offering and a sacrifice to God for a sweet-smelling aroma.

EPHESIANS 5:1–2

Now the purpose of the commandment is love from a pure heart, from a good conscience, and from sincere faith.

1 TIMOTHY 1:5

Now may our God and Father Himself, and our Lord Jesus Christ, direct our way to you. And may the Lord make you increase and abound in love to one another and to all, just as we do to you.

1 THESSALONIANS 3:11–12

And if you call on the Father, who without partiality judges according to each one's work, conduct yourselves throughout the time of your stay here in fear; knowing that you were not redeemed with corruptible things, like silver or gold, from your aimless conduct received by tradition from your fathers, but with the precious blood of Christ, as of a lamb without blemish and without spot. He indeed was foreordained before the foundation of the world, but was manifest in these last times for you who through Him believe in God, who raised Him from the dead and gave Him glory, so that your faith and hope are in God.

Since you have purified your souls in obeying the truth through the Spirit in sincere love of the brethren, love one another fervently with a pure heart, having been born again, not of corruptible seed but incorruptible, through the word of God which lives and abides forever.

1 PETER 1:17–23

Again, a new commandment I write to you, which thing is true in Him and in you, because the darkness is passing away, and the true light is already shining.

He who says he is in the light, and hates his brother, is in darkness until now. He who loves his brother abides in the light, and there is no cause for stumbling in him. But he who hates his brother is in darkness and walks in darkness, and does not know where he is going, because the darkness has blinded his eyes.

1 John 2:8–11

Therefore, as the elect of God, holy and beloved, put on tender mercies, kindness, humility, meekness, longsuffering; bearing with one another, and forgiving one another, if anyone has a complaint against another; even as Christ forgave you, so you also must do. But above all these things put on love, which is the bond of perfection.

Colossians 3:12–14

For you, brethren, have been called to liberty; only do not use liberty as an opportunity for the flesh, but through love serve one another. For all the law is fulfilled in one word, even in this: "You shall love your neighbor as yourself."

GALATIANS 5:13–14

But concerning brotherly love you have no need that I should write to you, for you yourselves are taught by God to love one another.

1 THESSALONIANS 4:9

GOD HONORS
YOU WHEN
YOU . . .

Take a Stand Against Worldliness

———————— ⚬ ————————

"No one can serve two masters; for either he will hate the one and love the other, or else he will be loyal to the one and despise the other. You cannot serve God and mammon."

MATTHEW 6:24

And do this, knowing the time, that now it is high time to awake out of sleep; for now our salvation is nearer than when we first believed. The night is far spent, the day is at hand. Therefore let us cast off the works of darkness, and let us put on the armor of light. Let us walk properly, as in the day, not in revelry and drunkenness, not in lewdness and lust, not in strife and envy. But put on the Lord Jesus Christ, and make no provision for the flesh, to fulfill its lusts.

ROMANS 13:11–14

Do not love the world or the things in the world. If anyone loves the world, the love of the Father is not in him. For all that is in the world—the lust of the flesh, the lust of the eyes, and the pride of life—is not of the Father but is of the world. And the world is passing away, and the lust of it; but he who does the will of God abides forever.

1 John 2:15–17

I beseech you therefore, brethren, by the mercies of God, that you present your bodies a living sacrifice, holy, acceptable to God, which is your reasonable service. And do not be conformed to this world, but be transformed by the renewing of your mind, that you may prove what is that good and acceptable and perfect will of God.

Romans 12:1–2

By which have been given to us exceedingly great and precious promises, that through these you may be partakers of the divine nature, having escaped the corruption that is in the world through lust.

2 Peter 1:4

"But take heed to yourselves, lest your hearts be weighed down with carousing, drunkenness, and cares of this life, and that Day come on you unexpectedly. For it will come as a snare on all those who dwell on the face of the whole earth. Watch therefore, and pray always that you may be counted worthy to escape all these things that will come to pass, and to stand before the Son of Man."

Luke 21:34–36

Now therefore, listen to me, my children;
> Pay attention to the words of my mouth:
> Do not let your heart turn aside to her ways,
> Do not stray into her paths;
> For she has cast down many wounded,
> And all who were slain by her were strong men.
> Her house is the way to hell,
> Descending to the chambers of death.

Proverbs 7:24–27

I say then: Walk in the Spirit, and you shall not fulfill the lust of the flesh. For the flesh lusts against the Spirit, and the Spirit against the flesh; and these are contrary to one another, so that you do not do the things that you wish.

GALATIANS 5:16–17

Then He said to them all, "If anyone desires to come after Me, let him deny himself, and take up his cross daily, and follow Me. For whoever desires to save his life will lose it, but whoever loses his life for My sake will save it. For what profit is it to a man if he gains the whole world, and is himself destroyed or lost?

LUKE 9:23–25

Beloved, I beg you as sojourners and pilgrims, abstain from fleshly lusts which war against the soul, having your conduct honorable among the Gentiles, that when they speak against you as evildoers, they may, by your good works which they observe, glorify God in the day of visitation.

1 PETER 2:11–12

Set Aside Your Pride

Pride goes before destruction,
>And a haughty spirit before a fall.
>Better to be of a humble spirit with the lowly,
>Than to divide the spoil with the proud.
>He who heeds the word wisely will find good,
>And whoever trusts in the Lord, happy is he.

PROVERBS 16:18–20

He who is of a proud heart stirs up strife,
>But he who trusts in the Lord will be prospered.
>He who trusts in his own heart is a fool,
>But whoever walks wisely will be delivered.

PROVERBS 28:25–26

Then Jesus called a little child to Him, set him in the midst of them, and said, "Assuredly, I say to you, unless you are converted and become as little children, you will by no means enter the kingdom of heaven. Therefore whoever humbles himself as this little child is the greatest in the kingdom of heaven."

MATTHEW 18:2–4

But He gives more grace. Therefore He says:
"God resists the proud,
But gives grace to the humble."
Therefore submit to God. Resist the devil and he will flee from you.

JAMES 4:6–7

"Yet it shall not be so among you; but whoever desires to become great among you, let him be your servant. And whoever desires to be first among you, let him be your slave."

MATTHEW 20:26–27

Hear and give ear:
> Do not be proud,
> For the LORD has spoken.
> Give glory to the LORD your God
> Before He causes darkness,
> And before your feet stumble
> On the dark mountains,
> And while you are looking for light,
> He turns it into the shadow of death
> And makes it dense darkness.
> But if you will not hear it,
> My soul will weep in secret for your pride;
> My eyes will weep bitterly
> And run down with tears,
> Because the LORD's flock has been taken captive.

JEREMIAH 13:15–17

"Take My yoke upon you and learn from Me, for I am gentle and lowly in heart, and you will find rest for your souls. For My yoke is easy and My burden is light."

MATTHEW 11:29–30

Choose to Speak Carefully

Death and life are in the power of the tongue,
And those who love it will eat its fruit.

PROVERBS 18:21

Let no corrupt word proceed out of your mouth, but what is good for necessary edification, that it may impart grace to the hearers. . . . Let all bitterness, wrath, anger, clamor, and evil speaking be put away from you, with all malice. And be kind to one another, tenderhearted, forgiving one another, even as God in Christ forgave you.

EPHESIANS 4:29, 31–32

Pleasant words are like a honeycomb,
Sweetness to the soul and health to the bones.

PROVERBS 16:24

He who guards his mouth preserves his life,
But he who opens wide his lips shall have
destruction.

"A good man out of the good treasure of his heart brings forth good; and an evil man out of the evil treasure of his heart brings forth evil. For out of the abundance of the heart his mouth speaks."

LUKE 6:45

"But I say to you that for every idle word men may speak, they will give account of it in the day of judgment."

MATTHEW 12:36

Whoever guards his mouth and tongue
Keeps his soul from troubles.

PROVERBS 21:23

As long as my breath is in me,
And the breath of God in my nostrils,
My lips will not speak wickedness,
Nor my tongue utter deceit.

JOB 27:3–4

Give to God's Work

———— ⁘ ————

Now Jesus sat opposite the treasury and saw how the people put money into the treasury. And many who were rich put in much. Then one poor widow came and threw in two mites, which make a quadrans. So He called His disciples to Himself and said to them, "Assuredly, I say to you that this poor widow has put in more than all those who have given to the treasury; for they all put in out of their abundance, but she out of her poverty put in all that she had, her whole livelihood."

MARK 12:41–44

But this I say: He who sows sparingly will also reap sparingly, and he who sows bountifully will also reap bountifully. So let each one give as he purposes in his heart, not grudgingly or of necessity; for God loves a cheerful giver.

2 CORINTHIANS 9:6–7

"He who is faithful in what is least is faithful also in much; and he who is unjust in what is least is unjust also in much. Therefore if you have not been faithful in the unrighteous mammon, who will commit to your trust the true riches?"

LUKE 16:10–11

Moreover he commanded the people who dwelt in Jerusalem to contribute support for the priests and the Levites, that they might devote themselves to the Law of the Lord.

As soon as the commandment was circulated, the children of Israel brought in abundance the first-fruits of grain and wine, oil and honey, and of all the produce of the field; and they brought in abundantly the tithe of everything. And the children of Israel and Judah, who dwelt in the cities of Judah, brought the tithe of oxen and sheep; also the tithe of holy things which were consecrated to the Lord their God they laid in heaps.

2 CHRONICLES 31:4–6

He who has a generous eye will be blessed,
For he gives of his bread to the poor.

PROVERBS 22:9

And let us not grow weary while doing good, for in due season we shall reap if we do not lose heart. Therefore, as we have opportunity, let us do good to all, especially to those who are of the household of faith.

GALATIANS 6:9–10

"Give, and it will be given to you: good measure, pressed down, shaken together, and running over will be put into your bosom. For with the same measure that you use, it will be measured back to you."

LUKE 6:38

Develop a Discerning Spirit

———————— ⚜ ————————

For this reason I bow my knees to the Father of our Lord Jesus Christ, from whom the whole family in heaven and earth is named, that He would grant you, according to the riches of His glory, to be strengthened with might through His Spirit in the inner man, that Christ may dwell in your hearts through faith; that you, being rooted and grounded in love, may be able to comprehend with all the saints what is the width and length and depth and height—to know the love of Christ which passes knowledge; that you may be filled with all the fullness of God.

EPHESIANS 3:14–19

Let us therefore be diligent to enter that rest, lest anyone fall according to the same example of disobedience. For the word of God is living and powerful, and sharper than any two-edged sword, piercing even to the division of soul and spirit, and of joints and marrow, and is a discerner of the thoughts and intents of the heart. And there is no creature hidden from His sight, but all things are naked and open to the eyes of Him to whom we must give account.

HEBREWS 4:11–13

He who keeps his command will experience
        nothing harmful;
    And a wise man's heart discerns both time
        and judgment,
    Because for every matter there is a time and
        judgment,
    Though the misery of man increases greatly.

ECCLESIASTES 8:5–6

To know wisdom and instruction,
>
>   To perceive the words of understanding,
>   To receive the instruction of wisdom,
>   Justice, judgment, and equity;
>   To give prudence to the simple,
>   To the young man knowledge and discretion—
>   A wise man will hear and increase learning,
>   And a man of understanding will attain wise
>   counsel.

PROVERBS 1:2–5

But the natural man does not receive the things of the Spirit of God, for they are foolishness to him; nor can he know them, because they are spiritually discerned. But he who is spiritual judges all things, yet he himself is rightly judged by no one. For "who has known the mind of the Lord that he may instruct Him?" But we have the mind of Christ.

1 CORINTHIANS 2:14–16

D0680575

THE NOON BALLOON TO RANGOON

A NOVEL BY

JOHN HAASE

SIMON AND
SCHUSTER
NEW YORK

25,620

To Peter, Tracy, Leslie
and Bobbie

THE
NOON
BALLOON
TO
RANGOON

1

. . . .

Precisely at eleven-forty-one on a sunny spring morning, Lady Trilby alighted from a crowded double-decker bus at Charing Cross Station, tossed a reprimanding look at her jostling fellow passengers, set the Royal Fusilier gait of one hundred twenty paces per minute, and headed in the direction of Whitehall to the British Foreign Office.

Lady Trilby, Lady Isabella Thorbush Trilby to be exact, was a highly respected member of the British peerage. Her late husband, Viscount Henry Thorbush Trilby, had fought valiantly alongside Lawrence in the deserts of Arabia. Though Lady Trilby would sometimes quote her spouse and recount his exploits in that war—"A bit hot . . . A bit sticky"—she was not a woman overly given to reminiscing. One simply had to get on with it, she would frequently remind herself after the Viscount's death, and it didn't *do* to court the past when the future was fraught with such fragility.

Though it was rather warm, she was attired in a sturdy tweed suit, and a rather floppy felt hat kept the sun out of her face. It was a good strong face and the periwinkle blue of her eyes gave an accent of youth, though each wrinkle and each chin—there were, alas, several of both—did not belie the full measure of her sixty-seven years.

Her life had been one of discipline and service, of many hardships and of the good breeding to suffer it well. She had traveled from pillar to post with her late husband and made homes in India, Burma, Ceylon and Kenya. She had raised two sons and lost them both— one to the wars, one to the Pope—and had seen one way of life give way to another and still another. Back in England she had watched her husband, a virile, heroic man, slowly retreat behind the amber curtain of a brandy glass, defeated not by wars but by a series of disastrous periods of peace. The dear Viscount expired of too much brandy and too little horse in the early days of World War II. Deemsgate, the family estate, was converted into an RAF hospital and Lady Trilby spent the war years in London, rolling bandages during the day and too often sleeping in the tube at night to avoid the dreaded bombings.

A hardy soul, she survived the great conflagration and, a bit grayer and a bit vaguer after the war, returned to Deemsgate to open its gates to tourists and their sixpence. But she soon tired of the chewing gum on the ancestral crests, the candy wrappers on her hearths, the snitchers, the palmers, the outright thieves who obviously felt that a little heritage in the flight bag was better than on the walls or floors of some musty castle.

Thus, having lost her family and what amounted to her home, she presented herself in the Foreign Office and demanded her ancestral birthright: an ambassadorship.

After much shuffling from one outer office to another, she finally reached the inner sanctum of Messrs. Warner and Banks, ensconced in baronial leather armchairs behind richly carved massive oak desks. The office they shared in the old wing of the Foreign Office had a pleasant fire roaring in the hearth, and the dark paneled walls were hung with crossed sabers, heraldic shields, brownish photographs signed by former prime ministers or renowned spies, and even a case of blue moon butterflies which Banks had once collected on an assignment in Sumatra. As Lady Trilby noticed the brandy on the teacart and the rack of pipes on the desks, the riding crop tossed on an ottoman, a pair of boots nearby, a hunting horn, she swelled with pride and thought, Yes, this is England.

Banks was the first to address her. He was a heavyset man, stocky but not gone to fat. His complexion was somewhat florid and his nose a little too bulbous, and these bore testimony that he was a man not too accustomed to self-denial. But there was no vulgar grossness to his figure or his face. He bore it all well, both the weight and the color, as if there were still much boy left in the man.

He had been a career diplomat for more years than he cared to remember and when a crisis arose nowadays, he found himself wishing for the old times when wars were fought with foot soldiers, rifles and cannon, when espionage still involved men dressing as women and vice versa, when good hotels like Shepheard's in Cairo and the Palace in Geneva served as reliable sources of information, and when the Orient Express invariably held enough secrets to keep a department such as his humming merrily along toward retirement.

But wars have changed and combatants are no longer the men with the guns, but the men with the slide rules.

Though Banks had always been known as an agent of great imagination and resourcefulness, his knowledge of matters scientific was quite scant. Even in a world of A-bombs, IBM missiles, computers and satellites, a birthright such as Lady Trilby's seemed to him more natural and proper. It gave him a nostalgic feeling for his own time.

"You say, Lady Trilby, that you are entitled to a diplomatic spot?"

"Quite."

"May we see your credentials?"

"Most certainly." Lady Trilby reached into her large knitting bag and produced a brittle parchment which she handed to Banks. He undid the faded blue ribbons gingerly and spread the ancient papers on the desk, took a magnifying glass out of a bottom drawer and started to read.

"What a marvelous hand," he said. "No such calligraphy left these days . . . marvelous, marvelous, look at these L's and the O's. Works of art! Works of art!"

Warner—a much taller, thinner man who looked like someone stepping aside to let a woman pass him in the narrow aisle of a sleeping car, a bit sheepish, half apologetic—was now leaning over Banks's shoulder and reading aloud. "The holder of this document shall be entitled to an ambassadorship, the locale of his own choosing, all countries, provinces, regencies, dukedoms, except Portugal—"

"Portugal," said Banks, "I wonder why." And then as he turned to the end of the document, he added, "Ah yes, Henry the Fourth, I should have guessed."

"Henry the Fourth? Portugal?" Warner scratched his sideburn with the mouthpiece of his pipe.

"I am afraid, dear Warner, you spent a bit too much time on the playing fields of Eton," said Banks, turning to Lady Trilby to share the joke with her.

"It was a minor affair," she said. "Perhaps not every history book recorded it."

"Perhaps. Well, Lady Trilby, your credentials are not only beautifully preserved, but in order. The world is your oyster. Where would you like to serve?"

"I have considered France," she said. "I do like their wines and I have a cousin there, a dear old lady, really; and Switzerland, I love the brisk walks and the good clean air—but my conscience won't allow such luxuries." She shook her head. "No, I must, after all, go where I feel I can best serve the Crown, and I've decided to go to the colonies."

"The colonies?"

"Yes. My late husband served as military adviser to a film company in Hollywood in the late thirties (*Pago-Pago,* a dreadful job), and he bought a house in Ramona Beach; it's still in the family and certainly can serve as the Embassy. The Viscount spoke to me of that house, the natives, their habits, their yearning for civilization."

"But," Warner said.

"But, nothing," Banks interrupted.

"You see India has fallen back into her old ways," Lady Trilby said, "and after India, America will follow. I know they made their bid in 1776, but they failed so monumentally. I'm certain they're going to try again. The Empire is shrinking. It's sad but it's true. Another

Dark Age is upon us. If you will prepare the documents, I shall pack my things and 'head for the bush,' to quote the late Viscount."

"Ramona Beach, you say?" Banks asked, and he thought he detected a little heavy breathing in Lady Trilby.

"Yes. Ramona Beach. I've seen enough of the natives in my home these postwar years. It shan't be an easy job to get them to stand on their own two feet, but then, I understand they're not very hostile."

She stood and bade the men farewell, and left as unceremoniously as she had arrived.

"The British Ambassador to Ramona Beach," Warner repeated. "Incredible. Tell me, Banks. I know I'm a bit weak on Henry the Fourth, but the Americans didn't fail in 1776, did they?"

"As a matter of fact, Warner, we were debating that question at the club the other day."

"Yes?"

"We came to the conclusion that it was conjectural."

A week later Lady Trilby returned and Warner and Banks had carefully assembled all the necessary diplomatic paraphernalia on the conference table. There was Lady Trilby's Commission, the British flag, the seal for the door and for her stationery. There was the code book, the *Foreign Service Manual* ("the Bible" as Banks said), *A Guide to the Americas,* and *Care and Feeding of Carrier Pigeons.*

"In charging you with this embassy, Lady Trilby," Banks said, "I should like—" He stopped. "May I speak informally?"

"Please do." She seated herself.

"As you know, England is a small island heavily dependent on its colonies for all we lack in abundance. It has not been an easy job over the centuries to keep the reins of Empire firm, but firm we've kept them." He leaned against his desk as he spoke. "I always think of England being clever and tactful. But tact must be handled very delicately. One can never throw it around lest one appear boorish. One can't even publicly profess it, for a braggart never fares well. I should say we've handled tact in the Foreign Office as the French use sauces—lightly, delicately, to bring out the flavor in one area or to suppress it in another. But the aftertaste should always be pleasant. Once a colony has left us, we would like to remain friends . . . it's a matter of survival."

"I understand perfectly," Lady Trilby said. "Spare the rod and save the child."

"Not quite," Warner spoke up. "I don't wish to quarrel with Banks here about the importance of delicacy, but I can't help stressing that a certain degree of firmness should be maintained. We can't afford to be pushed around. The sword should always be in evidence—sheathed, but in evidence."

"I am no mollycoddler, Mr. Warner," said Lady Trilby.

"I am not accusing you of that, my dear lady. I am merely trying to tell you that the Empire is behind you. Should you feel the need of strength, call on us."

"It's really rather simple." Banks smiled. "I mean, we do everything in the name of the Crown, it excuses a wide range of behavior, really."

"Yes, yes. Well, gentlemen, my ship is tugging at its moorings. It is a slow freighter, Japanese, but quite inexpensive. I shall study the manuals you have given me en route. I'll do my best."

"We're certain of it."

"I have one last request, gentlemen."

"Yes?"

"I am the last living member of my family. We're a hardy breed, but one never knows. Should anything happen to me, I should like to be buried on British soil."

"With all military honors," Banks said. "You have my word."

"Goodbye, gentlemen. God Save the Queen."

"Goodbye, Ambassador Trilby, and God speed."

The men handed the paraphernalia to Lady Trilby and showed her to the door.

"Oh wait!" Warner ran to the closet. "Don't forget the pigeons." He took out a cage with two gray, tired birds inside.

"What are their names?"

"Operator One-eleven and One-twelve. They're two of our best birds."

"I hope they like Japanese food," Lady Trilby said over her shoulder as Banks and Warner watched her walk down the long poorly lit corridor.

"Perhaps I owe you an apology, Banks."

"Whatever for?"

"At first I thought you'd gone completely mad when you sat there calmly asking her where she'd like to serve. She could have been Ambassador to France, good Lord, or Russia, Italy, the Vatican, the U.N. But the British Ambassador to Ramona Beach? Incredible. How did you ever know?"

"I didn't. It was simply Foreign Office tact to let her go on a bit. And now, my good man, we can say that Portugal's loss is Ramona Beach's gain."

3

. . . .

The *Hana Maru* stopped many times in its voyage across the seas before it reached exotic San Pedro, the last port of call for Lady Trilby. As she stood on the bridge of the weathered Nippon freighter, she watched the approaching shores of the promised land with a good deal of determination and a small dash of fear.

There was a lovely sunset; the air was warm and windless; San Pedro was pungent with harbor smells, the lights were going on in the houses on the hills, and the masts of hundreds of pleasure yachts and fishing boats were reflected in the calm orange waters.

"Well, Captain," she said as she stepped off the gangplank, "it looks peaceful enough."

"Peace proclaims olives of endless age," the Oriental gentleman replied.

"Confucius," said Lady Trilby (as if it were a salutation) and shook the sailor's hand and hailed a nearby taxi.

"Take me to a clean Christian lodging," she instructed the driver.

"I'll take you to the Tropic Palms," the cabby said. "It's real nice."

"It's really nice," she corrected.

"Oh, you've been there."

"Never," she said. "Make haste, I'm a bit tired."

They arrived at a lemon-yellow stucco edifice, its walls bordered by pulsating bile-green neon lights. A goodly part of the building was draped with enormous fish nets on which were affixed starfish and sea horses, leis, crystal balls from Japanese fishing grounds, miscellaneous crustacea, flora and fauna.

"This looks like an aquarium," Lady Trilby remarked, but the cabby delivered her to the office, unloaded her belongings, shrugged his shoulders and departed.

"I shall want lodgings for the night for myself and two birds," Lady Trilby announced to a rather ill-kempt young man behind the counter.

"We don't take no pets."

"We do not take pets," Lady Trilby corrected.

"That's what I said."

"You *said* 'We don't take no pets'; it's a double negative."

"O.K., O.K. What are you, a schoolteacher or something?"

"I am the British—" She stopped and prodded the boy's desk with her cane.

"Stand up!"

"What gives, lady?" The boy was more confused than angry, but he stood.

"Now, that's better, what does that say on your shirt?"

The boy looked at the stencil of his tee shirt. " 'Genuine Ford Parts.' It's a gag."

"I see. Very clever. Now, about the birds. They are not pets."

"No, what are they?"

"They're soldiers."

"Soldiers?"

"Yes. In the service of the Queen."

"The Queen?"

"Certainly you've heard of the Queen of England?"

"Sure, sure," the boy fumbled.

"Well, let's not dwell on that. Let's settle the room."

"What do you want? A studio? A single?"

"Just one bed will do."

"You want a double or a king or a queen?"

"I am afraid I don't understand."

"Gee, lady. You want a little bed or a big bed or a real big bed?"

"I am five foot six and a half inches tall," Lady Trilby

said, standing quite erect. "Do you have something that will fit me?"

"I'll give you Number Eleven. Come on, I'll show you."

She followed the boy past a series of cottages and finally he opened the door to a pleasantly furnished room. He turned on the lights, fully eight of them, next to the bed, in the dressing room, on the chiffonier, in the bathroom, and proceeded to demonstrate the prevailing amenities.

"The TV is over your bed and the controls are on the nightstand. If you watch the late late, keep it down. This button is the radio, and this one is for FM. Here's your phone and there's an extension in the bathroom, but watch it! If you want ice, dial four. It's free. If you're staying all night, there's complimentary break-fast in the morning, but don't worry about getting over-weight on it."

He stood in the middle of the room scratching his left ear. "I guess that's about it . . . Oh, if you want to have a ball, put a quarter in this slot." He pointed to a small receptacle mounted on the headboard. "It jiggles the bed for twenty minutes. It's kicksville."

Lady Trilby had removed her hat and sat quietly in one corner of the room. Like a seasoned traveler she had followed his instructions dispassionately. She reached into her purse, produced a coin and handed it to the boy.

"Fetch my things and draw my bath. I am ready to retire."

The boy pocketed the money and brought the lug-gage to the room.

"If you want to draw in the bathroom," he said before he departed, "you got to clean it up."

She bolted the door, undressed, bathed, and finally got into bed and turned off the lights. She closed her eyes but could not sleep, seeing thousands of youths, each stamped "Genuine Ford Parts." She saw her little birds dressed like Hussars and, unable to stand it any longer, she rose once more, fetched a quarter from her purse and deposited it in the little box above her bed. The bed rocked gently at first, but the vibrations steadily increased. She closed her eyes and thought of a Berber shepherd, though she could not explain why. Finally she raised herself slightly from her rocking bed and said quite discernibly, "Welcome to kicksville." Then she relaxed and dozed off quite peacefully at 75 decibels of sound and 140 revolutions per minute.

4
· · · · · · · · ·

The next morning she rose early and proceeded to Ramona Beach, eight miles north of San Pedro. It was a lovely drive along the Palisades. The proximity of the sea always cheers an Englishman. The Pacific looks quite formidable, she thought, but her mind was not so much on the scenery as on those pages of the *Foreign*

Service Manual which dealt specifically with an emissary's first days at a new post. She was rather ashamed of her behavior of the previous evening. She realized now she should neither expect the natives to sound like members of the House of Lords nor register horror at each new tribal custom. If these people existed on free ice and habitually massaged themselves to sleep, England might well be better off without them, but she acknowledged to herself that she shouldn't make hasty judgments. Thus, lost in thought and self-recriminations, she missed (perhaps mercifully) her first entrance to Ramona Beach and had to be told twice by the cabbie that he had brought her to the given address.

She looked out the window and saw a two-story home. It was quite pretty—Victorian, gee-gawed and gimcracked—and one sensed it had been designed by a good architect who had a feeling for the height of a turret, the width of a parapet. The entire structure was built of wood, once painted yellow but now giving way to the sea air. The trim was white and shiny as if it had recently been repainted. The house sat behind a waist-high iron fence bordered with nasturtiums and petunias in pots. A slightly sloping lawn led up to a front porch painted a spartan gray. A few aging wicker rockers graced the porch and a baroque barometer hung near the door; a pair of black rubber hipboots stood at the side of the entrance. Scrollwork abounded on the supports of the porch, in the eaves of the roof, and on the window frames. The door was large and in its upper half had leaded windows carefully draped with ancient curtains. A bougainvillea crept over the roof of the porch, and its reddish-purple flowers rivaled a honeysuckle bush, stands of marguerites, African daisy, a Magnolia tree in full bloom, gardenia and chrysanthemum. Over the front door a faded sign proclaimed *A. Sabella—Fish and Ships.*

"Are you certain this is the proper house?" Lady Trilby asked the cabbie.

"One-eighteen Beachwood Lane. That's what you told me."

"Let me see that deed again." She studied the document and then looked at the number over the front door and the two coincided. She was quite mesmerized by the beauty of the house, but then—

"What's this?" she gasped. "It's going up in smoke, fire, fire!"

"What fire? Where?"

"Can't you see? Do something. Organize a brigade."

"A brigade?"

"A bucket brigade." Lady Trilby had now jumped out of the cab and was trying to press some youths nearby into service, but as she pointed again to the thick clouds of smoke, she was startled to see a huge billowing orange balloon rising majestically above the house.

"Good heavens," she said, "a blimp." But before she could share her discovery with those about her, there was a most frightful explosion. One minute a huge orange balloon, a rather massive visual experience, hung in the air and the next minute there was an equally massive void. A plummeting wicker basket broke the spell. Lady Trilby rushed to the back of the house to offer succor to the stricken balloonist. It was not a pretty sight. Here he was, the poor man, trapped in his little wicker basket surrounded by yards and yards of colored shreds. He looked as if he had dropped into the middle of a huge birthday cake and was trying to fight his way out of the frosting.

"Here, here, are you hurt?" she cried.

"Don't come any closer," the man in the wicker basket yelled.

"Are you hurt?"

"No, no. Just don't come any closer."

Lady Trilby stood her post and watched as a man well past sixty extricated himself nimbly from a maze of manila and straw until he stood quite firmly on the ground. He was wearing dark denim pants, a pea coat, rubber-soled shoes and a little black knit cap, which he now removed.

"I didn't mean to be rude, but I've got to sift through all of this and see what happened."

"Your blimp popped."

"Yes. I'm quite aware of that, but it's not a blimp. It's a balloon."

"I should say it *was* a balloon."

The man looked rather sadly at the remains, turning almost full circle in disbelief. "I'm afraid you're right."

"And I'm afraid I'm a bit tactless." She extended her hand. "I'm Lady Trilby, forgive my bluntness."

"I'm Captain Sabella. Let's have a drink." He cupped her elbow firmly and propelled her past the wreckage and into the house. He stopped in the kitchen to fetch a bottle of wine and two glasses and motioned Lady Trilby to follow him to the parlor.

"Sit down, sit down." He uncorked the bottle and

filled two tumblers with wine, handed Lady Trilby one and raised the other.

"Here's to Chianti. I know *it's* lighter than air."

Lady Trilby looked around the room; it was sparsely but neatly furnished. The walls were whitewashed and the floor was varnished the color of a well-loved pipe bowl and covered here and there by hooked circular throw rugs. The furniture of mixed vintage and ancestry somehow fit. A Franklin stove stood against one wall and fading photographs in oval mahogany frames hung over a rolltop desk well-cluttered with papers, pipes, models of balloons and marine gear, a bit of chain, a belaying pin and a wooden pulley.

"This is good wine, Captain."

"It's from the Old Country, Genoese. Italian like me."

"I'm British," Lady Trilby said.

"Yes," Captain Sabella agreed and refilled their glasses.

"These are lovely goblets, Captain."

"Venetian. Did you say your name was Lady Trilby?"

"Indeed."

"I have some royal blood in my own veins, but it has been diluted by the waters of Venice over the years."

"Ah, Venice," said Lady Trilby. "What a fairyland."

"Yes," Sabella agreed rather mournfully, "before American Express took it over."

"I rather know what you mean; they have a branch in London too."

Sabella stared into the depths of his glass, speaking almost to himself. "I used to rise early. Venice is most beautiful at dawn, a gentle fog covering the canals like a blanket of gauze, all the color drained out of the water, the palazzos hovering in the air . . ." He was a handsome man. His hair was white, but full and gently waving. Dark piercing black eyes like ripe olives were set in his teak-colored face and a small well-trimmed mustache graced his upper lip. His frame was sparse, but solid; only a little roundness of his shoulders and the texture of his hands gave any evidence of his years.

"Well now, Captain, since we've divulged our ancestry, I wonder if you'd be good enough to tell me what you're doing here?"

"You British have always been a direct lot, haven't you?"

"I didn't mean to pry, Captain."

"You're not, dear lady. It's been so long since anyone has cared, I'm almost anxious to talk about myself. What can I say? The House of Sabella has been in Venice for over five hundred years and if you asked any native about the Sabellas all these many centuries, they would answer, 'The Sabellas, yes, a noble family. Retired aren't they?' I am the eighth generation Sabella that is retired. That is, I was. No one can even remember where all the original capital came from.

"The story goes something like this: A rich merchant once asked my great-great-great-grandfather to hold his satchel while he visited his paramour. My ancestor waited all through the night and most of the next day for the man to return, but he never materialized. The satchel contained a great fortune and the House of Sabella was on its way—"

"And you mean that generation after generation of Sabellas just lay about the house doing nothing?"

Sabella sat up a little straighter. "Not being engaged in a productive capacity is not an Italian's idea of doing nothing. If you English would only learn to sit still once in a while."

"You don't look like a man who is doing nothing."

"That is only a matter of necessity, dear lady. About ten years ago Grimaldi, the banker, visited me at lunch-time. 'Sabella, my friend,' he said, 'it is over.'

" 'What is over?' I asked.

" 'The money.'

" 'It can't be.'

" 'It has lasted five hundred years. You shouldn't complain.'

" 'But what shall I do?'

" 'Work.'

"I grew angry. 'Work. Work in Venice? No Sabella has ever worked in Venice.'

" 'Then leave Venice and work.' "

Sabella shrugged his shoulders. "So I left Venice and here I am. I skipper the *Louisa*. Best sportfishing boat south of Morro Bay. Six dollars a head. Leave at four and return at noon. No fishing Sundays."

"But what are you doing in this house?"

"It's my house," Sabella answered almost indignantly.

"It's *my* house," Lady Trilby said. "Look here." She took the deed out of her purse and handed it to the Captain. "Here, read it."

"No." The Captain held up his hand. "You read it to me."

"It is a grant deed made out to my late husband, Viscount Trilby, One-eighteen Beachwood Lane, Ramona Beach."

Sabella got up and walked to his desk. He fumbled through some newspapers and found a pair of steel-rimmed glasses, put them on and returned to his seat.

"Let me see that. Where does it say—oh, here, One-eighteen B. Beachwood Lane. One-eighteen *B*. Beachwood Lane."

"I'm dreadfully sorry." Lady Trilby now stood. "You mean there are two houses?"

"No. There is only one house."

"But . . ."

"There are two floors. This is one-eighteen A."

Lady Trilby sat down again, fanning herself with the deed. "Say no more." She pointed upstairs. "One-eighteen B."

Captain Sabella studied Lady Trilby, but she did not betray her emotions. Finally she stood up. "It looks as if the late Viscount has left me half a house."

Sabella still said nothing.

"Do you have the key for the upstairs premises?"

"Yes."

"May I have it?"

"Of course, but I should warn you. It is occupied."

"By whom?"

"The Stoltz brothers."

"And who may I ask leased them the property? My solicitors never informed me of any income from this house."

"There is no income, madame. No one has occupied that floor for years. The Stoltz brothers are learned

· 28 ·

gentlemen merely 'in residence.' They are a bit difficult but good German Weimar stock, you know the sort."

"Quite."

"They are scholars of a sort, writing the definitive history of elevators, 'lifts,' I think you English call them, and they're in a little financial difficulty." Sabella lit his pipe. "Once I was in the same predicament and the Stoltz brothers gave me money to keep working on my balloons. We're kindred spirits really. We have the same goal."

"What goal?"

"Ascension."

Lady Trilby reminded herself of the Service Manual and held her temper. "I don't mean to sound uncharitable, Captain Sabella, but I am not a rich woman. I am afraid I shall need all the space which is properly mine."

"I understand. Perhaps you would take one Stoltz brother and I could take the other?"

"You're forgetting propriety."

Sabella shook his head and smiled. "Italians have been known to . . . Well let's get you settled."

It is a testament to Lady Trilby's fortitude that she accepted the succession of events which had transpired in such a short time. No sooner had she learned that her house was really only half a house, than she discovered the unfortunate condition of the premises which were rightfully hers. The physical condition of the flat didn't bother her, for the Stoltz brothers, being good Germans, were the most meticulous of house-keepers. But the entire atmosphere was half Emmet half Kafka. Strewn about the upstairs rooms were vintage elevator cars, hoists, cables, ancient iron cages, directories, wiring, models of elevators, blueprints, tome-filled bookcases, desks strewn with elaborate drawings and projections.

To attract the attention of the Stoltz brothers, who were furiously welding in a corner of the kitchen, Sabella had finally to cut off the oxygen supply to their acetylene torches. As they raised their shields, Lady Trilby was somewhat surprised to see two very elderly gentlemen holding their torches like boys with faulty sparklers on the Fourth of July.

"Gentlemen," Sabella said, "I want you to meet Lady Trilby, your benefactor."

Both Stoltz brothers stood up rather militaristically and bowed from the waist.

"She has come here from England to take up residence in her flat."

"You have just come from England?"

"Yes, by boat."

"Have you been to the House of Commons lately?"

"Yes, why?"

"How is their pneumatic elevator?"

"I'm certain I don't know."

"We have heard rumors that there is a leak in the exhaust system."

"I have heard there is much exhaust in the House of Commons," Lady Trilby said, "but I've never known the cause."

One of the Stoltz brothers escorted Lady Trilby to a corner of the living room where there stood an amazing mass of dark metal. "This is an exact copy of an 1884 Blinot Elevator Car used by Admiral Foch after signing the Versailles Treaty."

"Well, that's very nice," Lady Trilby said. "But you'll have to put it and all those other things away and play somewhere else."

"But what are we to do? You're looking at twenty-five years of research."

"I am looking at very disrupted quarters and I shall thank you to give me the room which is my due."

"But have a heart, Lady Trilby."

"I have a heart, Mr. Stoltz."

"*Dr.* Stoltz. Heidelberg. 1904. Summa cum laude."

"I have a heart, Dr. Stoltz, and a rather robust physique, but it does at times require rest, and peace and quiet."

Lady Trilby left the men, their cages, and their dilemma and walked to the parlor. She stared out the window, not at the beach filled with people frolicking in the sand, but at the endless expanse of water and the spray and vigor of the surf.

Captain Sabella came up behind her shoulder and almost startled her with his question: "You're going to settle here?"

"Until my work is done."

"What kind of work?"

"Captain Sabella, I am the British Ambassador to Ramona Beach." At that, Captain Sabella retreated as quietly as he had arrived. He walked slowly down the steps and into the back yard to survey his ruptured balloon.

5

. . . .

The following days were busy ones for Lady Trilby.
Since the Stoltz brothers could not be moved overnight,
she put them to work fitting out the embassy. She affixed
the brass sign to her front door. It read:

THE BRITISH EMBASSY
OF RAMONA BEACH
ROOMS FOR GENTLEMEN
ESPIONAGE DONE

She had the Great Seal of the United Kingdom hung
over the parlor window and a sturdy flagpole erected.
Gradually she began to feel rather well disposed toward
the Stoltz brothers, who were not only helpful but un-
questioning.

It was no simple task to convert the quarters of two
elderly elevator buffs into some semblance of British
propriety and officialdom. The first thing, of course,
was to rid the rooms of their pastel colors, flowered
wallpapers, endless photographs of antiquated machin-
ery, and give the Embassy some feeling of solidarity
and permanence. Lady Trilby sanded all wooden
cornices to their natural finish and applied a dark oak
stain. She paneled the walls in mahogany or painted

them in good substantial colors of dark green, olive, dark brown or gray.

She divided the nine rooms into three portions: her own living quarters, an area for official business and an area which could be sublet for income. Top priority was given to the Queen's bedroom, which the Manual clearly stated should be provided by all embassies of the Crown should the monarch decide to repose for the night on a visit to the colony. There was no problem in designating a room as the Queen's, but the choice of bed was difficult. Lady Trilby did own one sturdy four-poster of Louis XIV vintage, a bed which had been in her family for seven generations and bore all the scars and patina of a much-loved piece of furniture. But she had planned to use this bed for her own. This left two single beds which she had brought from England. One would have to suffice for the Queen's chamber and the other for the guest room. The Manual said nothing about accommodations for a consort, and Lady Trilby pondered seriously the protocol of having to suggest to Prince Philip that he sleep at the Tropic Palms Motel. However, the thought of having to give up her four-poster, and the fact that Philip was, after all, a young and agile man made her decision simple. She could handle it, she knew, if they arrived together; perhaps the Prince-Consort might enjoy the massage at that. She would at least provide the necessary quarter.

She furnished all the bedrooms simply. Her room, facing the ocean, contained the four-poster bed, a good solid rocking chair, and a graceful mahogany side table with an ancient but pretty brass spy glass on its polished top, focused and at the ready. A marble-topped dresser held a porcelain washbowl and pitcher, a photograph of her departed husband astride Trigoff, his favorite gelding (also departed), and a bit of granite she had salvaged during the war from the rubble of Westminster Abbey to keep alive her memory of the bestiality of the Huns.

The parlor would serve as official territory and Lady Trilby used all her resources to give this room the proper British flavor. The furniture, though quite old and threadbare, was covered with heavy red and green velours, amply tasseled and edged in silks. The walls were hung with scenes of the English countryside, the Hunt, the Changing of the Guard at Buckingham Palace. She had the Stoltz brothers construct wall shelves on which she placed her collection of Toby mugs. One wall was lined with the family trophies, bearing testimony to much service and courage, medals and sabers, machetes, Hindu daggers, all the accouterments of years of military heritage.

The room was undoubtedly cluttered, with the British standard in one corner, the large grandfather clock in another, the brass umbrella stand near the door, the ottomans, the couches, the library table with its stacks of British periodicals, the teacart, the photographs of the Queens, Elizabeth and Victoria, in silver frames, the ones of Churchill, Eden, Attlee and Baldwin in passe partout, the large oil painting of Disraeli in the House of Commons and the even more massive one of Nelson at Trafalgar. And yet it all fit, like a well-made mosaic, to lend a touch of British nationalism amidst the stucco and the neon of Ramona.

One room off the parlor served as her office and contained only a small, almost dainty Chippendale desk and a high-backed leather-covered chair, the "telly," the decoding books and several reference volumes, *The Art of Warfare, Sign Language for Everyone,* and *Karate, a Manual of Self-Defense.* Here too she kept the hymnbooks which the Church of England so generously provided for all the outposts.

The remaining rooms she kept unfurnished and available for suitable boarders to help defray the cost of operations.

She and the Stoltz brothers had worked assiduously for several weeks, and when the last picture was hung to Lady Trilby's satisfaction, when each piece of furniture, each throw rug, each antimacassar and lamp, each crest and ornament had finally found its permanent position, she decided the day had arrived to open the Embassy officially.

There only remained the matter of polishing the brass plaque mounted on the front door, a simple chore which quite delighted her, when she saw Captain Sabella for the first time in several days. He was returning from work, a lunch basket in one hand, a straw-covered, dark-green wine bottle in the other.

"Captain Sabella," she called, "Captain Sabella."

He stopped and watched her labors with the brass plaque.

"Home is the hunter and all that," she said.

"Yes, all that. You seem to be quite busy yourself."

"This is the last remaining chore. After I've done this, would you join me in a little ceremony?"

Captain Sabella set down his lunch basket and his bottle of wine.

"Why of course. What are we celebrating?"

"It's a formal ceremony," Lady Trilby said. "I'd suggest you'd better get dressed."

"At this hour of the day?"

"Yes, and wear all your decorations."

"I'm afraid I can't get quite that dressed," Sabella apologized. "All my formal attire is still in Venice."

"Neatness is all that is required," Lady Trilby said and she and the Captain retreated to their respective quarters.

The ceremony began with scratchy recorded martial music emanating from a window in the Embassy. Lady Trilby had amplified the worn phonograph to its maximum, and whatever was missing in fidelity was certainly made up in spirit.

She descended the flight of steps from the Embassy wearing a dark blue dress, her ample chest crossed by a scarlet sash upon which various multicolored medals were displayed at random. The Stoltz brothers wore ancient, elegant cutaways. Their top hats no longer shone but gave signs of many years of repose in a moldy hatbox, yet they lent a certain dignity and charm. Captain Sabella honored the occasion by wearing a leather bow tie clipped to his buttoned denim collar, and though he did not wear any medals, he had put a large daisy into the top buttonhole of his heavy woolen cardigan.

Lady Trilby faced the men and the many small neighborhood children who had been lured by the music. Neither the Stoltz brothers nor Captain Sabella were quite prepared for what was about to transpire, but even in their brief acquaintance with Lady Trilby, they had learned to expect anything.

"Well, gentlemen," she said, fishing in her knitting bag for something, "this is rather an historic moment for Ramona Beach." She produced the Union Jack. "Yes, an historic moment," she repeated, "for we are about to witness the official opening of another embassy in Her Majesty's Service."

She stopped and looked at the rapt faces of the men. "I am somewhat emotional about all this and know I should say some fitting words. I searched the *Royal Nautical Almanac* all night for some stirring statement of Nelson or Trafalgar but I must confess I dozed off. Suffice it to say that at this moment it is high tide in Harwich, and up with the standard!"

She handed the flag to Captain Sabella and pointed to the flagstaff. The Stoltz brothers untangled the lines, Captain Sabella snapped the shackles to the grommets of the Union Jack, and all eyes followed the rising, fluttering flag. Lady Trilby reached into her knitting bag, produced a vintage breech-loading flintlock, and fired into the air.

"It's not a cannon," she said apologetically, but the surprised and somewhat shaken men quite agreed that "a salvo is a salvo" no matter what its source.

6

. . . .

Ambassadors the world over are judged quite severely by the quality of their reports. It is one thing for a man to be the eyes and ears of his country, and another for him to commit to paper what the eyes have seen and the ears heard. One man may be given to literary embellishment, another extremely reticent and cool under fire; some humorous, if not frivolous; some more than slightly alcoholic and delusionary. Since one man's wolf may be another man's tiger, it is extremely important to know how to read the reports of the men in the field. Impending hostilities may move one ambassador to say, "Armageddon is at the gates," another, "It looks a bit sticky," while a third may report, "Embassy on fire, suspect trouble." It is quite vital, therefore, for the Foreign Office to know their diplomats' style. There was one thing both Banks and Warner agreed on: Lady Trilby had a style all her own.

> The British Embassy
> Ramona Beach, California
> *By Diplomatic Pouch*

Messrs. Warner and Banks
The Foreign Office, Whitehall

Gentlemen:

I have traveled enough in my lifetime to understand that first impressions are usually erroneous. I should like to state therefore that some of my comments should be taken with a grain of salt. Give me a little time to acclimate and things will seem less immoderate.

The situation in the colonies is much more desperate than I had ever suspected. One gets such a distorted point of view living in England and seeing the American natives tour our National Monuments, brandishing their Japanese cameras, their Diners' Club cards. In England they certainly *look* civilized.

But here, in their native habitat, one does get another picture of them and it is not a happy one. I can look out my window right this minute and I can state categorically that 80 per cent of them are shoeless, and their clothes, thought not in a bad state of repair, are minimal almost to the point of indecency. Granted, the weather is mild at this time of year, but I shudder to think of the impending fall and winter.

Their eating habits are equally appalling. They seem, poor dears, to exist on nineteen-cent hamburgers, on tacos (some sort of Mexican confection), chili dogs, frosties, freezes, Cokes, Pepsis, malts, a native brew known as "Salty Dogs" and similar comestibles. I think they aim to freeze their taste buds, which no doubt helps to stave off the hunger pains. They are all terribly lean and have marvelous teeth, I must say. I recall the Swahili tribe in Kenya exhibited the same phenomena.

As a matter of fact, I have often thought of the Swahili tribe since I've been stationed here. The drums go all night (they call them bongos). The women wear golden shoes and do strange things with their hair; some have it streaked, others have two heads (of hair) —imagine, wearing a false one right over the natural one—many of the native women have paintings on their knees, and a goodly number of them wear trousers, while many of the males seem to walk about dressed only in a towel. I don't quite yet know what they *do*. Mostly, I observe them lying about the beach, but with their low caloric intake one can't go about prodding them to be useful. First things first.

Efforts should be made to feed and clothe these people. Speak to the Minister of Agriculture about surpluses. Anything will do really—a porridge, some sort of warm gruel, meal mush, just fill their little bellies. As for clothing, perhaps the military has some surplus. Start some sort of drive to get English ex-servicemen to donate their cast-off uniforms. We must cover their bodies for more reasons than cold. I shall get off a letter to the Archbishop of Canterbury. The Church has specialists in covering breasts, and all that sort of business, I understand. They've had quite a lot of success in the tropics.

Well, I don't mean to sound like a bleating old woman. We *are* doing things here. I have started a little garden of radishes, potatoes, leeks, onions; the bulletin board has been mounted and I have been exhibiting various views of Britain: the Tower of London, Stratford on Avon, Big Ben, the Beefeaters—that's been a popular photograph. I admire the work that the Duchess of Windsor did in Nassau teaching the native women to weave baskets, and I have been looking for some indigenous material to help these people along, but the only things in abundance are beer cans and bottle tops and I don't see a ready market for this as yet.

I am sending along some snapshots of the Embassy. You will notice that it is *upstairs* (a personal mishap), but we are located above a Venetian balloonist, a rather solid gentleman—and some German gentlemen building an elevator in the back bedrooms.

Sincerely,
Lady Trilby, Ambassador

Pigeon follows with details.

> **ϡ**
> · · · · · · · ·

Lady Trilby's concern with her new charges prompted her to continuous activity. But her very physical approach to things, to dive rather than jump, to run rather than walk, to use a cane where a finger would suffice, really camouflaged an inner turmoil. The hundred pounds allowed her by the Foreign Office could not begin to keep her alive even at the most favorable rate of exchange. She had planned to rent rooms to proper Englishmen but even an ad in the Ramona Beach paper:

WANTED
Gentlemen, British
Good Christian Habits
No Harpists Allowed

produced only a phone call from the Anti-Defamation League.

One should remember that Ramona Beach was hardly an average little town, even before Lady Trilby arrived. Since it was primarily a resort community, it had a full complement of bizarre establishments to amuse both its residents and visitors. There were coffeehouses and discotheques and Ramona-a-go-gos, model raceways, bowling alleys, miniature golf courses, fly-by-night art galleries, astrologers, cryptographers, palmists, chiropractors, herbalists, all in their separate edifices, flag bedecked, neon bordered, bold arrows, pointing hands, revolving lights, amplified recordings, almost a permanent circus. It is little wonder that neither Lady Trilby's Union Jack nor her rather impressive bronze plaque ruffled anyone. No one took her seriously. The few that passed by might have wondered when she would open her shop and what she would have to sell.

Her anonymity might have prevailed indefinitely were it not for the unfortunate arrival the following Sunday morning of the ignominious "Sweethearts" motorcycle gang.

Lady Trilby had as usual attended church and was slowly walking home enjoying the relatively well-scrubbed look of the parishioners as they slowly made their way home on a fine sunny morning. It was perhaps ten after twelve when she suddenly found herself alone on Ramona Boulevard, a street which only a minute before had been well populated by churchgoers and those heading for the beach. The natives' practiced ear had recognized the frightening sounds of a hundred motorcycles as they swept down the road from the Palisades, and they had scurried for shelter.

Little wonder, for the Sweethearts were the roughest, toughest, dirtiest, meanest collection of men, whose only passions were their high-powered motorcycles, beer, and the destruction of public and private property. Like all bullies they attacked only small towns whose defenses were too weak or ineffectual to present any challenge. They swept down like locusts, attacked, raped, bullied, stole, destroyed and departed, leaving a swath of destruction like a Midwestern tornado. Only the litter of beer cans remained.

And thus they rolled into Ramona. Policemen quickly called in sick, shopkeepers closed their stores, the highway patrol took to the highways (in the other direction), only Lady Trilby remained, slightly confused and terribly exposed.

It was a strange confrontation. A hundred young bums, sitting on their spewing cycles, unkempt and unshorn, unshaved and unwashed, a hundred hoodlums wearing black leather jackets and jeans, goggles, gloves, boots, swastikas, iron crosses and an incongruous red heart like a valentine embossed on the back of their jackets. A hundred men and a lady who walked from cycle to cycle commenting on a chromed piston, a jeweled saddle, the reverse curvature of a handle bar.

"Marvelous," she said, "simply marvelous. Don't you look fierce, my word, boys, make them roar, make them *roar*." Even the Sweethearts were somewhat confused by this fearless old lady and this mutual admiration might have continued had not one of the cyclists started to lift Lady Trilby off her feet and onto his motorcycle, yelling,

"How about a ride, grandma?" But no one touched the Lady's person lightly. She caned him down quickly and effectively.

"Don't you dare touch me until you've bathed."

The sight of one of their own defeated was all that was necessary to trigger the bedlam for which the motorcyclists had come. After some quick deploying of their cycles, Lady Trilby found herself totally surrounded by the little monsters.

"I am glad you're drawing closer, it is difficult to speak over the roar of your engines. I have a marvelous idea."

"What's that?" one of the monsters said quite sarcastically.

"You do so remind me of Knights of King Arthur, proudly astride their chargers. I'm wondering, have you done any jousting?"

"Jousting? What's jousting?"

"My word, you don't even know what it is? Well, in days of old the bravest horsemen, the knights, well armored, just like you"—she patted a boy's helmet and jacket—"would mount their horses, the fastest, finest horses in the land, and line up in rows on the lawns of their monarchs. There they sat, poised, straight as an arrow, their armor and their horses' armor gleaming just like the chrome of your motorbikes. Straight in the saddle"—Lady Trilby demonstrated—"holding a twenty-foot lance in their stirrup, perhaps a standard fluttering from its peak."

"Big deal, these guys just sitting on their nags holding a flag."

"Not a flag, a lance. On the signal of the huntmaster the horsemen lowered their lances, goaded their animals and *charged*. What a beautiful sight, fifty horsemen on each side galloping full speed against their opposing numbers, men and steel, and horses and standards and blood. What do you say?"

"Whaddaya mean?"

"Well, are you going to show your mettle or are you going to beat up a defenseless old woman?"

"I don't dig you, lady," one of the cyclists said. "Where you goin' to get all the lances?"

"Over there," Lady Trilby said, spying a pile of sewer pipes. "They'll do just fine. Let's borrow them. They'll make excellent lances."

"Wait a minute, wait a minute," another boy said. "What are we supposed to do—line up across each other?"

"Yes—three hundred paces."

"Then what? Just hold those sticks and *scrunch?* Where are the kicks?"

"You don't seem to understand at all. Firstly we divide you into teams." She removed her hat and unwound the silk ribbon from the brim and divided the violet silk into small pieces. Then she distributed the ribbons to half the cyclists. "Those with ribbons shall be the A team, the Hussars; the ribbonless, the B team, the Grenadiers."

"Now then," she continued, "we shall find an arena, the beach, yes, the beach will do very well, and we must get people to cheer."

"Cheer what?"

"The victors, of course, those are the 'kicks.' Imagine the pride you'll have in yourself and your machine if you survive unscathed."

The Sweethearts were in an obvious quandary, caught between historical ignorance and a clear challenge to their manhood, but Lady Trilby left no room for indecision as she started to roust the natives out of their homes, yelling, "Jousting—there'll be jousting at the beach."

Someone later remarked that she looked very much like the Pied Piper of Hamelin leading the Sweethearts and an ever-swelling mob of citizens to the main beach. It was Sunday, after all, and any outdoor spectacle was better than watching the endless breakers of the Pacific roll to shore.

Lady Trilby relegated the spectators to the dunes above the beach and carefully paced off the proper distance for the respective teams, and one had to admit it was quite a spectacle to see a hundred cyclists astride their fierce idling machines, holding twenty-foot lengths of sewer pipe. She picked one from each team to be captain and gave them final instructions.

"I shall," she said, "be master of the tournament." She reached into her knitting bag and produced her trusty breech-loading pistol.

"I shall fire once, which will be your signal to ready your steeds. I shall fire a second time and you will lower your lances. The third shot will be your signal to charge. Do you have any questions?"

The two team captains looked at each other in bewilderment and rage and gaped at the ever-growing crowd of spectators lining the foothills of the beach.

"I guess not."

"Well then," Lady Trilby said, "instruct your team and Good Hunting."

A hush fell over the audience as they watched the two opposing teams, astride their motorcycles, poised and ready, their right hands accelerating their engines, their left hands clutching the twenty-foot sewer pipes. A blue haze of exhaust covered the field of battle like early morning fog on Hampstead Heath. They watched Lady Trilby raise her pistol and listened to its report signaling the first charge.

The boys put their motorcycles in gear and headed for their opponents. Chaos ensued. Unaccustomed to their new weapons, unable to keep the long poles level, many soon embedded one end firmly in the sand, and hurtled like master pole vaulters in graceful circles into the air while their unmanned cycles shot out from under them like frightened rabbits. Others tangled their lances in the spokes of their opponents' motorcycles, turning the carefully polished chrome wheels into semblances of Calder mobiles.

Motorcycles collided and meshed, fused, tandemed and sideswiped each other until the scene resembled a view through a kaleidoscope.

No battle in Arabia, no skirmish of Rommel in Africa, could have held the color and the fury of the Sweethearts and their sewer pipes. Scores of young men grouped and regrouped to charge scores of other men who were merely trying to straighten their lances or machines. Some kicked their mutilated Hondas, or beaten crippled Yamahas, like angry cowboys urging their frightened mounts in the midst of a stampede.

Here was a lonely soldier looking at the remains of his once marvelous machine, with hardly enough of it left to hang on a watch chain, while thirty feet from him there lay three young men with motorcycles so hopelessly entangled not even a team of expert mechanics could have restored their machines.

And everywhere was Lady Trilby, dear Lady Trilby, cheering them on, coaching, encouraging the few mobile, undamaged riders to charge—charge—charge— once more to make a molten pyre out of their masterpieces of chrome and steel and rubber.

There was not a dry eye among the onlookers, nor an unhoarse voice. The spectacle had outdone all the jalopy races, the Indianapolis 500, pro football, or bullfighting, and all the genteel sports which demand much of the contestants and but a touch of lust from the spectators.

When day ended and they folded their blankets, gathered their empty Coke bottles and stray children, and looked on the beach below them and surveyed the Sweethearts dazed and battered, their motorcycles and their clothes in shreds, their helmets and goggles battered, there was no doubt that every citizen knew there was a British Embassy in Ramona and knew who was its Ambassador.

8

. . . .

The fact that one old lady was able not only to turn back but practically annihilate a hundred threatening motorcyclists earned her the undying gratitude and renown of all the citizens of Ramona Beach, all except the elected officials, the police force, the fire department, the highway patrol.

"Where were the cops?" men asked in barber chairs and at the lunch counters. "What kind of protection we payin' for anyway?"

"Didn't see old Mayor Taft around anywhere."

"Heard he was in Vegas when it all broke loose."

"Why didn't the fire department turn the hoses on those hoodlums?"

But the Mayor rather than ignoring the angry blast of the citizenry, soon mobilized his powers and tried to remedy the embarrassing situation by harassing Lady Trilby.

When the papers had finished covering the story of the Sweethearts, there were certainly many unanswered questions. Was this a genuine Embassy, and if so, what was it doing in Ramona Beach? Did Captain Sabella have a permit to fly balloons in a residential area? Did the building code allow steel elevators in a two-story wood-frame house? And what about this espionage business?

Mayor Taft's forces soon descended upon the property. The health department, the building department, the police and fire departments measured, wrote reports, and used all available instruments of officialdom at their disposal, but to Mayor Taft's chagrin, all of it was futile. The Embassy was indeed a bona fide embassy and therefore British soil, and Lady Trilby was a bona fide ambassador and consequently entitled to diplomatic immunity.

Seeing all his efforts turn to water, the Mayor resorted to a well-known American political device, namely labeling the whole complex a Communist plot. But even this failed to agitate the beach community. Ramona Beach seemed such a long way from Russia, particularly during summer, and with the World Series coming up invasion hardly seemed imminent.

Since Lady Trilby had not yet found a suitable handicraft for the natives to pursue, she felt it wise to begin some indoctrination.

"One can't just let them run around barefoot and half naked," she said to Captain Sabella one balmy evening. "I must get them moving in the right direction."

Sabella, grateful for having his launching pad protected by the Crown, was in no mood to contradict her, and he heartily agreed that a small sign on the bulletin board would attract attention.

"LADIES OF RAMONA," the sign read. "This is to announce the formation of the Afternoon Society. Get Acquainted Party. August 1st. 3 P.M. Tea will be served."

It was, however, no little surprise when forty women ranging in age from their late thirties to their early seventies arrived in a large bloc. Lady Trilby herself was somewhat taken aback when she saw so many, but she rose to the occasion and accommodated them as best she could around her parlor.

"Let's start with 'The Trooping of the Colors,' " she said, moving to an old phonograph and placing an even older record on it. "A rousing clarion piece. Music always rather gets people into the mood, don't you think?"

Lady Trilby obviously did not ask questions to receive any answers, for she put the recording on quite loud and seated herself next to an elderly woman who was busily taking notes. Glancing about the room, she noticed many of the other women equally busy writing in little black notebooks, and when the music stopped she rose and commented, "I'm really pleased you are a serious lot. I appreciate the notes you're taking. Now then, before I start," she said, rubbing her hands quite vigorously, "is anyone very hungry or very cold?"

She looked about the room but no one spoke up. "Very well," she said, "but I don't want any of you to be afraid of me." (At this there was a frenzy of note-taking.) "I am, it is true, wearing the sword of Empire," she said, "but it is sheathed," remembering Banks's statement at the Foreign Office. (This produced even more furious scribbling.)

"Since you are the first ladies to visit me, I want you to feel welcome and I shall depend on you to be my emissaries. We are all in this together, and the sooner we clean up this mess the better."

The ladies nodded energetically.

"The first thing, of course, is proper dress." She looked about the room and beckoned to an older woman dressed in a severe black dress, a choker about her neck, and a chaste black felt hat.

"Would you mind standing?" The woman was properly embarrassed.

"Me?"

"Yes. What is your name?"

"Spencer."

"Don't you have a Christian name, Spencer?"

"Abigail."

"All right, Abigail Spencer, stand up."

The woman stood rather feebly and looked at her compatriots with embarrassment, but Lady Trilby walked over to her, grasped her firmly by the shoulders, and made her face the room.

"Now I would say Abigail Spencer is properly dressed. She looks like a lady in the afternoon. A dark-colored dress, good solid walking shoes, I don't even object to the little ornamentation about the neck. We're not Zulus, but we *are* women. Sit down, Abigail. Women wearing trousers, long, short or medium is of course taboo," she continued. "There are parts of our anatomy which are best hidden by the stays of a sturdy corset. I have a marvelous woman if you want her name. As to bosoms, my attitude has always been that of Queen Victoria. 'They're there,' she said, 'but so is Lichtenstein . . . and they bring out enough commemorative issues.' "

Lady Trilby had the inimitable talent of being able to insult impartially, for there were indeed a few women in the crowd who wore mini-skirts, capris, slacks, bell bottom trousers, brightly colored sheer silk blouses, bikini tops and the like, but Lady Trilby spoke on as if she were addressing countless unseen masses from a balcony at Buckingham Palace.

She looked at her watch and then thought of the Service Manual and decided that it was perhaps unwise to burden these people with too much the first time.

"We shall meet here every Thursday at three P.M. exactly. Do try to be punctual. I have requested supplies from the Ministry and hope to have them here shortly, and we shall soon all set to work with our thimbles and needles. You do have them, don't you? Well, I seem to have done all the talking, and I think now I should hear from you. Don't be shy. Speak up. Do any of you have any ideas, suggestions, anything at all to help in our common plight?"

One graven woman stood up and said in a burst of hostile words clearly memorized for such occasions, "I would like to inform you that every woman in this room is a paid up member of A.G.A.I.N.S.T. A.G.A.I.N.S.T. (Americans, Good Americans, in Search of the Truth) is proud to be known as 'the moral vacuum cleaner of our country.' It is composed of an administrative group of older women known as the Againstgirls and a company of militant young men known as the Againstroopers. Its aims are clearly set forth in the *Yellowbook*, (available soon to the public). A.G.A.I.N.S.T. is an ideological society dedicated to the memory and the cause of its martyr-founded Arthur Maple, Junior, who died of self-inflicted hiccoughs in protest of the Communistic infiltration of Little League Baseball." She paused, took a deep breath and continued, "A.G.A.I.N.S.T. is unilaterally opposed to Catholics, Jews, Negroes, Lutherans, Baptists, Communists, Alaskans, blue-collar workers, the common cold, cellophane, Chinese, Japanese, Balinese, Greeks, Italians, detergents, recorders, mixed drinks and mixed dancing, First Ladies, Yosemite National Park, Lake Michigan, tea (in bags), vending machines, the Irish, ball-point pens, mail-order houses, federal penitentiaries, locusts, hummingbirds, tweed, body stockings, the Isle of Wight, turkeys, Alfa Romeos, social security, helicopters, triplets, whales, Connecticut, ringworm diseases, beer in bottles, Hindus, rodeos, nickel, cobalt, aluminum and fluorine gas. We are proud that our opposition to fluorine gas has brought us notoriety. Our members firmly believe that our Enemy is flooding our American air with fluorine fumes and so we Againsters can be easily recognized carrying our individual cylinders of Againstair strapped on our backs or carried inconspicuously in purses (one can for a dollar ninety-eight). Every hour on the hour, Againsters flood their lungs with this special gas to flush the poisons out of their system. A.G.A.I.N.S.T., madame, is America's sole hope of survival."

"Hear, hear," Lady Trilby said, quite amused, but the woman continued undeterred. "My co-workers have been taking copious notes, as you may have noticed, and we have already counted twenty-one infractions."

"My word," Lady Trilby said, still amused, "twenty-one infractions, that's enough for capital punishment."

"That won't be necessary," the woman replied. "You're killing yourself with that Commie air you're breathing."

"Perhaps I should apologize for breathing," Lady Trilby said, "but it's a bad habit the Trilbys have had for years."

The women stood on signal, closed their notebooks and marched out. "We shall be back next Thursday."

"Very well," Lady Trilby said, "oh, you forgot to drink the tea."

"We may wear pants," one woman said, "but we're not fools."

Lady Trilby stood at the door of the Embassy and said to herself, Refuse tea? What savages! She was relieved to see Captain Sabella approaching. He held up a rather pretty dead fish.

"Yellowtail. They're running. How about joining me for dinner?"

"How is that Genoese wine holding out, Captain?"

"Just fine."

"Well, if you'd let me bring dessert, I'll just feed my birds and get my intelligence off."

"I'll see you in a little while," he said and let himself into his quarters.

Lady Trilby soon joined Captain Sabella and they both puttered about his kitchen preparing dinner with a mutual expertise in things culinary and that pleasant lack of self-consciousness at the difference in their sex, which age brings. When the sauce was finally simmering and the fish properly baking under a blanket of thyme, cheese and paprika, they settled in his parlor and enjoyed a glass of port.

"How is the blimp, I mean the balloon, faring?"

"Almost ready for ascension. Just a few seams left to sew."

"How does a man get interested in balloons?"

"It's a long story, Lady Trilby."

"I don't mean to be personal. Heavens, my husband liked to crochet and another gentleman I knew once had the largest collection of streetcar transfers in the world—his name was Percival." She sank back in her chair and stared into her glass. "He always said, 'There is something immortal about a transfer—no end of the line.' "

"How can I explain the balloons," the Captain said. "The Sabella family has never been productive, but it was always musical. Several years back I had finished a profitable fishing season and was looking for a good reed instrument. One of the local papers had an advertisement for a bassoon. It has a lovely sound. My uncle was quite proficient. I drove to the address given in the ad and found, to my dismay, that the poor man's ad had been misspelled. He was selling a balloon. Not a bassoon."

"For shame."

"Well, as it turned out, the balloonist was also quite musical. A long discussion and much wine ensued. At three o'clock in the morning I quite agreed with his reasoning that it was really quite unfair of him to share my love of music when obviously I did not share his enthusiasm for free flight. So I bought his balloon."

Sabella busied himself bringing food from oven to table and continued his story.

"I knew all along that something was awry in the barter, but I was fortified by the fate of my cousin. He had been a pharmacist in Chicago and bought a drugstore at the height of the Depression. During a blizzard the D of the drugstore sign fell off, and since he was unable to pay for its repair, he found himself continually apologizing for not having any rugs for sale. When he found the demand for carpeting greater than that for Bromo Seltzer, he converted his operation from a pharmacy to flooring and died a happy man. I expect the same fate for myself. I am a devoted balloonist. The thought of being borne by the air makes a man accustomed to being borne by the sea feel a bit heady. Can you understand this?"

"Yes. How high have you been?"

Captain Sabella shrugged his shoulders apologetically. "About twenty-five feet so far. Something always goes amiss, but the potential is there. I dream of floating in the great Jet Stream, the Canary Islands, Taiwan, Rangoon ..."

"Is it not strange," she said, "that men of all ages are bent on some form of escape? Women, on the other hand, will cling forever to a few delicious hours in their lifetime, shoring up the later years like book ends on a treasured volume."

"We all work out the years the best we can," Sabella said. "Take the Stoltz brothers."

"What do you mean, take the Stoltz brothers. *I've got them*. At the rate they are dismantling their toys, I'll never be rid of them."

"I'll speak to them. They're not very practical men."

"I'm sorry for being querulous, Captain. There's so much to be done after all."

"Can I be of any assistance, madame?"

"Oh no. It just seems that a few volumes have slipped

in between the book ends lately. I think I'll rise an hour earlier and take a brisk walk on the beach. I do miss the moors . . . It was a lucky thing the man didn't have a baboon—wouldn't you say?"

Thomas and Pamela White were a typical young American couple. Thomas, a nice-looking chap, athletically lean, easily six feet tall and seemingly two feet wide in the shoulders, was a rather studious man despite his pro-ball proportions. A graduate architect from Stanford with an internship at Taliesin West, home and school of the late Frank Lloyd Wright, he had a critical eye for the world about him and a steady hand with the drafting pen to set it right. His wife, Pamela, was a columnist for *Panorama,* a weekly picture magazine with a circulation in excess of five million readers. They were bright, healthy, in love with each other and life in general.

The only problem in their seemingly idyllic union was the discrepancy in the remuneration which their respective professions provided. Pamela earned three times as much as Thomas, since *Panorama's* huge circulation could afford outrageous salaries and partly because architecture is traditionally a difficult profession in which to get an economic foothold. Pamela, being a sensitive girl, was upset by this inequity, but she had a flair for the dramatic and was convinced that if she could locate her husband's office in some bizarre atmosphere, it would help to attract more clients. She had almost succeeded in securing quarters for Thomas in a Chinese fortune cooky factory, but the proprietor withdrew at the last minute. She found a rather picturesque spot over a carousel in an amusement park, but Thomas feared that the constant music of the steam calliope would tend to put too many curves into his work. She kept looking for exotica, however, and it was little wonder, that after the A.G.A.I.N.S.T. meeting none other than Pamela rang Lady Trilby's doorbell.

Lady Trilby had been busily restoring the Embassy to its original state of confusion when she heard the chimes. She opened the door and recognized one of the women who had just attended the meeting.

"My name is Pamela White," said her visitor.

"Yes, I recognize you from the meeting today."

"You did? I came in disguise. I think you were simply marvelous."

"Really," Lady Trilby said.

"Do you *know* whom you entertained?"

"I thought they were just some native women."

"You practically had the entire Ramona chapter of A.G.A.I.N.S.T."

"The entire chapter, isn't that jolly."

"Hardly jolly, dear lady, they're a dangerous lot."

"Dangerous, my dear girl, pish tosh. Come join the Captain and myself in a spot of tea."

Pamela sat down after the introductions, and Lady Trilby asked why she had returned.

"I was doing a story for *Panorama*. I'm a columnist."

"A writer, I see. I've been rather plagued by writers since that motorcycle episode. It's all been a bit trying. I've asked all of them to mention that I rent rooms, hoping that some of the publicity might be fruitful."

"That's why I am here."

"You want to rent a room?"

"We would like to rent about three rooms."

"We?"

"Yes. I am married. My husband is a struggling architect. He covets this house. He calls it a good example of California Victorian."

"The dear Queen should hear this blasphemy. She'd turn in her grave if her skirts wouldn't get ruffled."

"We need three rooms. A drafting room for him, a living room and a bedroom."

"I had hoped to rent the space to Englishmen. A bit of home away from home, you understand?"

"Yes." The girl stood, a little disappointed, and proffered her hand. "Thomas, my husband's name is Thomas, knows nothing of this. It was all my idea. I was just trying to help him."

"Well, that is very commendable. You look like a spunky little girl. I like that. I do need the income. Yes, you and your husband are welcome to move in."

Lady Trilby's decision to have the Whites lease a portion of her quarters was based on several factors. One, she needed the money; two, it would be pleasant to have a little youth about the house; and three, she felt that it might be helpful to have some natives right under her roof. Surrounding herself with Englishmen, even if there were any about, might just make the Embassy that much more insular and lessen her chances of understanding the prevailing problems.

However, it had been a good many years since Lady Trilby had been so close to youth, and after the Whites had been with her for a few weeks she realized that she had forgotten that not all energies at that age are channeled into physical affection or work or play.

"All right," she heard Thomas yell one afternoon, "go ahead. Go on! Art for art's sake. Run around half naked. I don't give a damn. I don't give a good God damn."

"I'm not designing mixed sauna baths," Pamela yelled back.

"Well I am. Maybe we could tie in. 'Topless Waitress Swears by Mixed Sauna Bathing.' How's that for a lead?"

"You make me sick, Thomas. Do you think I like being a topless waitress?"

"Would you like to know the truth?"

"Go on."

"All right, Pamela. I think you like it. Yes, and I think you enjoyed being in a submarine for three days with one hundred and one men and twelve officers."

"*And* Admiral Rickover, don't you forget Admiral Rickover."

"And what about that week in the Marine boot camp, where was the Admiral then? And that *haircut*. Why don't you do a story on a nudist camp or a whorehouse —why go halfway?"

"Why go halfway, isn't that one of *your* lines? The

only way to rent bachelor apartments is to put in *sauna baths. Mixed sauna baths.*"

"If you know a better way to fill apartment houses, you tell me. Nobody's interested in closet space or double-burner ovens any more."

"And *Panorama* readers are not interested in casseroles or pruning rose bushes or happy little marriages. So there."

"Because there are no casseroles, and no roses, and no happy little—hell."

They both looked up to see Lady Trilby standing at the door.

"It's teatime," she said and walked to the kitchen. The Whites looked at each other rather sheepishly and followed their new landlady.

"I am terribly sorry," Pamela said. "I'm afraid we were disturbing you."

"Nothing of the sort. I love good healthy banter." Lady Trilby spoke and puttered about the stove, and finally produced a batch of cookies and a teapot and they all sat down in the parlor.

"We are a bit tight in here," she said. "Mind you, I am not a meddlesome old lady, but you must learn to modulate your voices. What is a topless waitress?"

"No top." Pamela demonstrated.

"Poor dears, and mixed sauna baths?"

"No bottom." Thomas demonstrated.

"*No* bottom," Pamela yelled.

"Please." Lady Trilby held up her hand. "It's teatime."

Thomas had been pacing the length of the parlor, but finally sat on the davenport next to Lady Trilby.

"I know," he said quite soberly, "that all this must sound like absolute and utter nonsense to you."

"One should not judge, may I call you Thomas?"

"Perhaps," he continued, "it's all my fault."

"A bit of chivalry is always welcome. You don't need to explain anything."

"Yes. I'd like to. Architecture is a tough game for a young man. One either works for a large firm as an employee, which stifles all creativity, or one strikes out for himself, which stifles all income." Thomas was wringing his hands self-consciously. "I have all sorts of ideas for office buildings, public structures, university work, but every builder asks the same question: 'Have you ever built an eighteen-story building or a hundred-and-fifty-thousand-square-foot structure?' and I always have to say no. All the big commissions go to the same number of architects."

"How do you survive?"

"I have a talented wife."

"Don't say that Thomas, you're busy."

"Yes," he said bitterly, "building an endless number of dull stucco apartment houses."

"I'd hardly call them dull, Thomas."

Thomas turned from Pamela and looked at Lady Trilby. He said quite somberly, "I believe in an honesty of design."

"Bully, Thomas."

"Take bachelor apartments. Let's analyze them. For the owners, the object is to crowd as many tenants as possible into the least amount of space at the highest prevailing rate."

"Well put, Thomas," Pamela cheered.

"For the tenants, it is to provide the greatest accessibility to the quarters of the opposite sex. I have just finished one building, two hundred singles, The Pill on the Hill. There are no doors on the apartments at all. That was a considerable saving. The apartment house offers mixed sauna bathing, sunbathing, free judo lessons."

"Also mixed," Pamela added.

"Yes, and the usual amenities."

"Like bathrooms and kitchens?" Lady Trilby wondered.

"No, swimming pools, weekly luaus, no-host cocktail parties, over-the-hump parties, a sports car clinic, a resident analyst."

Lady Trilby shook her head in unison with Pamela, who prodded Thomas.

"Tell her what the new apartment house is called?"

"The Nursery," he said almost proudly.

"Isn't that too much?"

"You've got to create an image," Thomas said.

"Whatever do you mean?" said Lady Trilby.

"You're British, right?"

"Quite right."

"Now ask me what kind of image that projects?"

"What kind of image does that project?" Lady Trilby asked, quite dutifully.

"Why, a man in a bowler hat, a stiff collar, carrying an umbrella, wearing a trenchcoat, yes, and of course a bushy mustache."

Lady Trilby's face fell. Never before had she heard of such an outrageously synthetic Englishman. "*That* is the British image?" she queried.

"Yes, wouldn't you agree, Pamela? Like that fellow we've seen poking around the embassy grounds lately."

"Definitely."

"*Say no more,*" said Lady Trilby.

She rose and walked to a bookcase in the corner of the room, searched for a specific volume, found it. She seemed quite excited suddenly holding the volume in front of her. "Now then," she said, "let us strike a bargain. You two read this book. It is Lord Cromwell's *History of the British Isles*. He's a bit stuffy but a well-informed patriot. Do that for me and do nothing about these headless waitresses and these sauna baths." Then she waved them off. "Back to your regiment. I must be about my work." Ten minutes later she was busily writing her report to the F.O.

The British Embassy
Ramona Beach, California

Gentlemen:

Whatever wheels you are setting in motion, I don't know, they are either square or traveling in reverse. I have received neither food nor clothing, and the need, gentlemen, is acute. Do you realize some of the poor waitresses must work without the benefit of any clothing on top. Can you imagine the sort of trouble this can bring about?

I have instituted the Afternoon Society and about forty native women attended. They were a serious lot, and I've begun the course of manners and morals. Poor dears, they seem quite xenophobic, but as long as they *care* about something I suppose there is some hope.

Now about this espionage business. I *did* read the

Service Manual and quite fully understood it: "Information valuable for the defense and safety of the Empire should be transmitted post haste to the Foreign Office." The meaning is quite explicit and I do not want to quarrel with it, but I hardly consider it *British* to be underhanded about the thing. If you demand espionage, so be it, but one can hardly instill trust in the natives as it is. You must remember, they have nothing to hide. Why with the little they wear I'd scarcely wonder *where* they'd hide anything.

But to my astonishment there seems to be a dangerous character about, an impostor, a false Englishman, who has been seen snooping around the Embassy. All I can discover so far is that he wears a bowler, a trenchcoat, and an umbrella, which is always a suspect combination, and he hides himself behind a bushy mustache. There is something in this which certainly sounds conspiratorial to me, and I fear it may be a "cover" (as you people say) for something truly dreadful; but I can't yet put my finger on it. I shall investigate.

Hurriedly,
Lady Trilby

Pigeon follows with details.

10

. . . .

The next day was Thursday and Thursday meant another meeting of the Afternoon Society, but before it
was held, Lady Trilby set about to confront the ever-
present Stoltz brothers, whose intentions may well have
been honorable but whose performance was certainly
lackluster. Try as they would they could not really
muster in Lady Trilby any enthusiasm for their efforts.

"Right here is a perfect replica of one of the first
water pressure elevators built in India. You can see this
tank," Dr. Stoltz explained, "it was filled with water.
The weight of the water lifted the cage."

"I understand, Dr. Stoltz."

"When the cage reached its top elevation, the water
was released and the car descended."

"Fascinating."

"Of course, the passengers on the down journey got
drenched."

"Really?"

"But the builders got around that problem."

"How?"

"They provided oilskins for the descent."

"Here," he continued, pointing to another Oriental

gilded cage, "is a replica of the elevator of the Imperial Plaza in Chungking. Complete with the bullet holes of the Three Tong Wars."

"I am sure this is all terribly fascinating for some people, but I need this room. I shall want to lease it. I can well use the funds. Things are a bit short commons."

"Can't you arrange for some sort of subsidy? A Guggenheim, a Rhodes scholarship. After all, you *are* the British Ambassador."

"If it were in my power, sir, I might be inclined to assist you."

"We'll dedicate the history to you."

"That is very touching, but nothing in my Service Manual provides for this sort of exigency."

"In that case, Lady Trilby, we shall vacate the premises."

And they kept their word. They succeeded in dismantling their last elevator, removed their torches, cylinders and the tools, and cleaned and painted the rooms which they had occupied. But to say that the Stoltz brothers had departed would be erroneous. They had indeed vacated Lady Trilby's premises, but not until they had obtained her permission to build an elevator in the back yard.

"Well, you know it is only half my back yard," she said to them. "You must check with Captain Sabella. He does fool around there with his balloon."

"We have checked with him, and he has agreed that we could build a five-story elevator on the northeast corner by the avocado tree. And, Lady Trilby, it is not just any elevator. It is the pièce de résistance of mechanical ascension! The Great Steam Elevator of the Plaza

Athenée in Paris, the finest example of baroque elevation."

"Yes," the other brother added. "Red velvet tufted
seats, a summoning bell which plays in the octaves of
Bach the Elder."

"Four bud vases filled with roses."

"A glovebox for the operator's spare white gloves."

"A cage to rival the Taj Mahal in its grace and
beauty."

"You want to build a five-story elevator to what?"

"You don't seem to understand, Lady Trilby."

"No, I don't think I do."

"We are just building a five-story elevator. A shaft
and a car."

"Going to what?"

"What do you mean, 'going to what?' "

"Well, I have always thought that lifts transported
people from elevation to elevation."

"Oh, that's incidental."

"Is it really? If you built the shaft next to the house,
it would save me a lot of steps."

"And you could make a cocktail table out of the
Mona Lisa too. An elevator is a thing of beauty—nothing seems to convince you of this. A fusion of steam, gas,
hydraulics, of electricity, grace of motion, quiet, swift—
safe. Do you realize that elevators hold the record for
passenger safety?"

"Wasn't there a huge disaster in the Eiffel Tower?"

"Oh a few drop here and there, but the averages are
phenomenal."

"Fancy that. Then you're just going to build an elevator. A five-story elevator going nowhere?"

"Yes, it's never been done, you know. It will be the first *pure* elevator in history."

"Tell me," Lady Trilby said. "How does a man get interes—" She stopped.

"I beg your pardon," one of the Stoltz brothers said.

"It's nothing," Lady Trilby said. "Nothing. The last time I asked that question, somebody told me about baboons."

But Lady Trilby had other duties, and she set about preparing for her ladies. They appeared promptly at three o'clock replete with notebooks, little American flags, and she could not help but notice the improvement in their dress. One can well imagine the surprise of these devoted patriots as they entered the door of the Embassy and found Lady Trilby on the floor of her parlor confronting an enormous stuffed boar.

There was, of course, an explanation for this striking phenomenon; it originated in Lady Trilby's penchant for hunting. It had always been a part of her way of life; she possessed a good eye and a steady forefinger. But there were many other titled Englishwomen who rode to the hunt with distinction. Lady Trilby gained her extraordinary renown by becoming one of Britain's foremost amateur lady taxidermists, no mean feat. Her rare talent allowed her to fix and mount each carcass in its most menacing pose, and the mobility of her life with the Viscount afforded her innumerable opportunities to fill Deemsgate with tigers, cheetahs, leopards, lions, panthers, even a full-sized rhinoceros which had taken a full year to stuff. But, in retrospect, taxidermy might well have been the cause of much hardship in Lady Trilby's life, since that particular hobby initiated one of those typical marital problems which had no beginning or end. Those who loved the late Viscount were aware that the presence of the animals in his home often perturbed him.

"How would you like to get up and see them all in the middle of the night?" he used to complain to his friends in the club. "Why just to get to the W.C. I've got to pass a leaping jackal and pass under a pouncing tiger, and I'm forced to share the privacy of the bath with a mounted school of piranha."

"It's dreadful, sir. Dreadful."

"It is, Malcolm. I swear they're alive . . . it's their eyes. Their eyes glow in the dark!"

Lady Trilby took quite a different attitude. She felt that fear in a soldier was quite out of character, and in public she swore that her husband saw animals no matter where he was. She loved to tell the tale of the prince who had been so afraid of gunfire in his youth that the royal governess was instructed to fire a pistol in the young boy's room after he had fallen asleep to harden his auditory nerves. It should be added that Lady Trilby was not aware of this story's outcome: When the prince reached manhood and the throne, he stuffed his ears with cotton, shot the governess in her sleep, married a pretty barkeep, abdicated and manufactured music boxes.

The climax of this marital strife came late one night. Hoping to cure her husband once and for all of his foolishness, she had managed to sneak a small live leopard into the bedroom. As the dear Viscount maneuvered toward the four-poster, he slipped easily between the cheetah and the lion, but when the leopard, lying in front of the dying embers of the open hearth, yawned peacefully, the poor man set a new local record by leaping from the casement in an unparalleled broad jump across the family moat.

One of the most precious objects Lady Trilby had brought to Ramona Beach from England was an unfinished boar's head. She had shot him in Broadbent and mounted him in Moorhead, but it had taken all of four months for the firm of Hillinghand and Bentley to ship a proper set of glass eyes for the animal. Thus Lady Trilby was discovered on the floor with the head and the shipment of glass eyes by twenty frightened ladies.

"Isn't that a fierce yellow," she said, pointing to a glass eye that glinted in the sun. "Hah, the fight never goes out of a good eye."

The ladies shrank back in horror, but Lady Trilby quickly stood up and patted the beast with the head of her cane. "Don't step on him, ladies, I've had a devil of a time collecting these." The warning was hardly necessary.

"Come, come," she said, "let's continue what we were about."

One of the A.G.A.I.N.S.T. ladies promptly stood and addressed her.

"We have had a Secret Konklave and there are some questions we want to put to you."

"Sally forth," Lady Trilby said.

"How do you feel about socialized medicine?"

"Capital. Absolutely capital." She removed a rather too pink upper denture, waved it about the room and not until she reinserted it was she able to tell the ladies, "This set of teeth is the best thing Clement Attlee ever did for dear old England. I have another pair made under the Wilson regime and there's not nearly the quality of workmanship. They don't have the bite, would you like to see?"

The poor A.G.A.I.N.S.T. ladies, who had barely recovered from the eyes about the floor, were now thrown into new fits as Lady Trilby waved her false teeth about the room. But she soon restored order and persuaded her guests to seat themselves in a circle about the room.

"Well now, don't we look better. Sit down, sit down. I've chosen to begin with the music of Rimsky-Korsakoff today. Something lusty about those Russian peasants, don't you know?" Again there was much scribbling by the ladies as her worn phonograph painfully reproduced the sounds of the Leningrad Symphony Orchestra.

"Now then," she said after the music ended. "I had hoped to have material at hand today to begin on sewing, but the wheels of Empire grind slowly, so we shall devote our time to the study of government."

"Hear, hear," the ladies remarked.

"I am always reminded of Lord Wallace's famous remark that Statecraft is better than working. It is therefore best always to be suspicious of anyone in the community who aspires to the body politic. I state quite categorically that close investigation will show that ninety-nine per cent of all politicians' characters are flawed. They have either failed in business, they have discovered that it is easier to talk than to work, to sit rather than stand, ride rather than walk. They are little men who gain stature by office or men unloved who seek mass devotion."

Thus far there was no quarrel between them.

"Of course there have been exceptions—Churchill, Disraeli, Gandhi, even that Eisenhower fellow seemed like a hard-working chap."

"Now wait a minute, wait a minute." One woman stood up, apparently unable to contain herself. "I'll go along with your theory about politicians. The less men in government the better. The less government the better. One good patriot will suffice. But don't you speak of men like Disraeli, or Eisenhower—not to us. We know. We pay *dues,* we're informed about the Red Menace."

"The Communists," Lady Trilby began, but she lost her audience as Captain Sabella floated serenely by the open window and all the ladies stared in amazement.

"Good afternoon, Captain," she called out. To her surprise the ladies huddled in little frightened groups, whispering, "Did you see? Right by the window, a Captain, we're surrounded, it's a plot."

"Ladies, ladies, please, it's only Captain Sabella." But her visitors were now panic-stricken, edging away from the window, and if there had been any chance of quieting them down, of calming their fears, of explaining Captain Sabella, the ensuing explosion turned panic into bedlam and propelled the ladies toward all available exits. The brief reappearance of Captain Sabella as he made his unplanned, unfortunate descent, and the sight of the Stoltz brothers (themselves frightened by the noise) trying desperately to fight themselves out of one of their elevator cages left a deep and lasting impression on the ladies as they gained freedom of the street. Now they were sure. The so-called British Embassy was a most dangerous Communist cell and Lady Trilby a crafty enemy who must be done away with.

But Lady Trilby's immediate concern was not with the hasty departure of her guests but the welfare of poor Captain Sabella, who was rushing toward her at the same time she was rushing to him.

"I know, I know," he said, "my blimp popped." But there was an enormous smile on his face. "I actually cleared the roof today. Must have been up thirty feet, thirty-five at least."

"You're bleeding," said Lady Trilby, pointing to his forearm.

"Oh, it's nothing, merely a scratch. I think I'm really getting the hang of it. Only another ten feet and the off-shore breezes would have taken over."

"I should really be very cross with you, Captain. You frightened the poor natives so, I doubt if they'll ever come back." But there was a smile on her face.

"Good riddance. Those women are nothing but a bunch of troublemakers anyway. Come, I'll take you on a spin on my ship the *Louisa*. The ocean is lovely this late in the afternoon."

Lady Trilby accepted the invitation happily, feeling the need for some air after a stormy day.

The *Louisa* was a sturdy thirty-year-old double-ender originally built to work the waters of San Francisco Bay. Double-planked mahogany with a teak-apitong stem and masts made of hollow spruce, she was forty feet long and sixteen feet wide and carried twelve paying guests and a crew of two, Captain Sabella and his helper Alfonse. The Captain's territory was the flying bridge that sat somewhat precariously atop the cabin and was reached by a narrow iron ladder. Captain Sabella could scarcely conceal his wonder at Lady Trilby's agility in reaching this perch to stand beside him. He started his trusty diesel and watched the blue smoke of the exhaust pouring rhythmically from a narrow steel funnel behind the bridge.

"Would you like me to cast off, Captain?"

"No, I'll do it. You seem to know your way about boats."

"Heavens yes. You forget I'm British."

"Not very often." Captain Sabella laughed as he descended the ladder, let go the lines and gently walked the *Louisa* out of her berth. Then he mounted the steps again, threw a well-worn brass lever into the forward position and gently eased the boat into the channel leading to the sea.

He set the throttle to a steady eight knots and both of them watched *Louisa*'s bow cut a frothy slice into the blue waters of the Pacific.

"That's Catalina across the channel." Sabella pointed due south. "And that's Point Conception, see the lighthouse?"

"Yes, indeed. Tell me, Captain Sabella, the name *Louisa,* was that your wife's name?"

"It *is* my wife's name."

"You mean you're married?"

"Didn't you know?"

"Certainly not."

Captain Sabella laughed heartily. "I'm married to the *Louisa.* If a man has a good boat, he doesn't need a wife."

"You're jesting with me, Captain."

"I am indeed, Lady Trilby." He leaned back and put one foot on the rungs of the steering wheel and his free arm about Lady Trilby. "Would you like to marry me?"

"Well, that's a most charming proposal, dear Captain, but I'm afraid you're quite a happy man."

"I am," Sabella confessed. "Just think, all day long I make my living purveying what all these poor souls save up to enjoy once a month—a little fresh air, a live fish, a little peace from the wife and the kids. I am happy until I look down from this bridge and see Alfonse the deck hand."

"Really, what's so special about him?"

"He enjoys the very same sea and the very same air without the burdens of command, the hazards of private enterprise."

"Still your income is greater than his. You've confessed your weakness for silk foulards, an occasional massage."

"Actually, Alfonse's income is greater than mine."

"Then you're too generous."

"It's not me, Lady Trilby. On Thursdays he practices psychoanalysis. That pays thirty-five dollars an hour, eight hours, well you can imagine."

"You mean he is a proper doctor?"

"No, his brother is."

"I'm afraid I don't understand, Captain."

"I know it's confusing. They are identical twins. On Thursday, Alfonse's brother likes to go fishing, so Alfonse puts on his brother's suit and takes over the office patients, and his brother serves as deck hand on the *Louisa.*"

"But how can a deck hand treat patients?"
"That's not the problem; psychoanalysts just listen."
"I see. Then what's the problem?"
"His brother is a lousy deck hand."

11

Since the Stoltz brothers' only worldly desire was to write the definitive history of elevators, and they asked nothing more from their fellow man than a little peace and a little room to pursue their goal, one could hardly call them evil men. However, things were quite otherwise with the notorious real estate developers, the Gutter brothers. It is, of course, unfair to chastise men whose only goal in life is to make money. Who knows, but that their very names, Walter and Willi Gutter, might have prompted their quest for wealth? But no one in Southern California would deny that they had gotten significant mileage out of their slogan, "From the Gutters," which has graced countless real estate developments, tin and copper mines, oil wells and many other interests too numerous to mention. And so it came to pass that the Gutters eventually came to Ramona and met with Mayor Taft.

"Mr. Mayor," said Walter Gutter, "I don't think you

quite understand the economic benefits we can bring to Ramona Beach."

"Quite frankly I don't," the Mayor said, his hand out, palm up.

"Our figures show," Gutter continued, "that a retirement community pumps real lifeblood into a town. These folks spend."

"Well, they may," Mayor Taft admitted, "but *you* don't quite seem to understand the complexion of this city. It is a beach town. The accent is on youth, fresh air, vitality. Our chief attraction is the beach."

"Very true, Mayor, very true. And beaches attract not only youngsters—we have found that oceans, mountains, lakes are all conducive to the mood of the old folks. Besides what do these youngsters spend their money on? Hamburgers, bathing suits, motor bikes, beer, comic books."

"I don't see where the retired spend their money? Most of them have fixed, limited incomes."

"They're bums," Willi Gutter now spoke up.

"Who is?" Mayor Taft asked a little startled.

"Everybody is."

"Well, now, I wouldn't go that far."

"Excuse my brother, Mr. Mayor. He is a pragmatist."

"I don't know what that means," Willi Gutter said, now standing up and pushing his brother into the chair which he had just vacated.

"Look, Mayor, my brother likes to beat around the bush. I don't. Retirement communities are like any other tract. For every five hundred homes you need a shopping center. An A and P, a department store, drugstore, a post office, a movie house. Get it?"

"Yes, I get it."

"Now we don't make a lot on the houses, but we make it on the shopping centers."

"None of this is news."

"That's right. Except there is one added goodie in the retirement game. The funeral parlor." He stopped pacing. "That's the plum. Get it? There's not *one* decent funeral parlor in Ramona Beach. Why should there be? You got all these kids running around here, making them healthier and healthier."

"I didn't know that was a crime."

"Who said it was a crime? Motherhood isn't a crime either, but it's not listed on the New York Stock Exchange."

"Well, gentlemen, let me give your proposal every consideration," Taft said, now standing, but Willi Gutter was not a man to be put off.

"We've already given the proposal every consideration and it makes sense. We want you to rezone the following blocks." He walked to a grid map of the city. "From Avenue B to Avenue L, northwest and from Ocean Front to Lomitas Street north south. This means leveling some thirty houses, a junior high school, a laundromat, a couple of nursery schools."

"Now wait a minute!" Taft shouted.

"We can't wait. We're just finishing The Hope of Heaven tract in Newport Beach: one thousand homes, three parlors. The Never Too Late tract in Oxnard is almost completed, six hundred homes, two parlors. That heavy equipment has got to roll—get it? Dozers, scrapers, fillers, compounders. My God, you politicians are all the same."

"What do you mean?"

"You're impractical. Haven't you ever thought about the economics of death?"

"Dead men don't vote," Taft said.

"That's true, but think of it. Half of the people in this country are of retirement age. You can't just leave them scattered all over the countryside dying piecemeal."

Taft shook his head but said nothing.

"You've got to collect them, herd them into retirement communities. That's the only way you can make a funeral parlor pay. Supply and demand."

"Isn't all this a little cruel?"

"We've all got to go," Gutter said. "Business is business."

"You're so full of clichés," Taft said, "you sound like a politician yourself."

"I agree, there's much too much talk. I want action, Mayor. What do you say?"

"All right." Taft finally put his hand in his pocket. "You're blunt. I'm blunt. What's in it for me?"

"Two things," Walter Gutter now spoke. "You're coming up for re-election in two months. We'll finance the campaign, the whole thing. Buttons, bumper stickers, air time, barbecues, all the rest of the shenanigans and"—he held up his hand—"a piece of the parlor."

"Just imagine, Mayor, on a warm summer day, you'll be able to walk through that great development and feel you've got a little piece of every resident you meet."

"Real community spirit, wouldn't you say?" Willi Gutter laughed for the first time.

"I want you to put in a bid to the American Funeral

Parlor Society to hold their convention here. I want a good modern aggressive parlor to come into Ramona. These people have to be *sold* on the community. They're not about to put a memorial chapel next to a Whiskey-a-go-go. Those electric guitars drown out the organ."

"Anything else?" Mayor Taft asked.

"Well, could you use an extra bathroom?"

"Why?"

"On the last tract we built, there's one left over."

"Damned plumbers roughed in a complete bathroom on a lot which isn't supposed to get a house."

"I don't think I could use one."

"Well, one of those pop artists said he could make a sculpture out of it."

"Bunch of bums," Willi Gutter said.

"Who? Artists?" Walter asked.

"Plumbers, artists, all of them."

The Gutter brothers left Mayor Taft slightly dazed. It was true that he had never given a thought to the economics of death, but he no longer questioned the morality of the issue. After all, he *was* up for re-election, and a wise politician does not question the conscience of his backers. Reluctant to press his own conscience, he looked out the window and watched Lady Trilby below him on the street causing her usual midday traffic tie up.

Lady Trilby piloted a handsome fire-engine-red electric golf cart; a round Japanese umbrella shielded her from the midday sun. The cart had a three-horsepower motor which produced speeds up to eight miles an hour on smooth downhill terrain. It sported an equally lovely shofar, a fine kerosene lantern on its bonnet and a sign on its rear fender which read, "If you're traveling faster than me, you're driving a motorcar. Repent." An unnecessary admonition, for no one could possibly pass Lady Trilby on the narrow streets of Ramona, and her diplomatic immunity left the local police helpless in dealing with the problem. The reverberations of the traffic jam came up into Mayor Taft's office, and his thoughts about the British Ambassador were anything but politic. He turned from the window with a sigh and returned to his desk. He had to extend that invitation to the funeral people for their convention, a dreary business, but next week would be the Surfers' Convention and the prospect of all those bronzed bikinied bodies cheered him a little.

Two events took place in Ramona Beach simultaneously the following week: the Surfers' Convention, and Lady Trilby's annual grippe. This grippe was not a blocking of nasal, sinus or bronchial passages, nor a particular slowdown or speedup of any other bodily functions, but rather a general leavening of a very active, hearty soul, much like the lay-up of a boat in the yard, the drying of a mainsail after a stormy crossing.

During these periods Lady Trilby took to bed complete with mustard plasters, leeches (if available), alternating hot and cold packs, much brandy in water glasses, and a general attitude of helplessness and depression, not aided this year by contemplation of her role in Ramona, her accomplishments, or lack of them. After all, the natives were still ill clothed and ill fed and spent much of their time lying on the beaches. The Afternoon Society had collapsed and there were still no supplies forthcoming from England.

Tucked, swaddled, bandaged, mustard-plastered, ice-packed, and lying meditatively in half-darkness, Lady Trilby was quite unaware that one of the signal events of the year, the annual Surfers' Convention, was beginning all about her. The invasion into Ramona of the surfers has a seriousness and orderliness not unlike a meeting of the American Society of Cost Accountants as the surfers register at the Ramona Biltmore, giving their names, the size and weight and composition of their boards, signing up for an endless number of events and competitions leading ultimately to the Championship of Surfing held at the "Cove" slightly north of the city where the surf is higher and of the "curl" or "hook" type offering skilled surfers a "clean slide" not unlike Canoe Surf in Waikiki.

The similarity of the Surfers' Convention to other conventions ends however at the registration desk, since no believer would deign to live in a hotel room. Indoor space is complete anathema to this hardy breed of sportsmen. They eat, sleep and play entirely on the very beaches which afford them their challenge. Armed with nothing more than their boards, perhaps an extra pair of trunks and a towel, they are indeed Nature's children, bronzed, lean, their hair bleached by the sun and the sea, and when they are not engaged in their sport, they are busy lying about the beach, listening to rock and roll, talking about the great surf of Sunset Beach at Oahu, the Cunha Surf, Makaha Beach and the legendary heroes of their sport: Dave Heiser, "Rabbit" Kekai, "Blue" Makua, Sarge Kalanamoku, "Chukie" Salzman.

Ramonans liked the surfers. They were a clean-cut, trouble-free lot on the whole, too exhausted or too well mannered to raise havoc in their city after sunset, and the week might have passed into surfing history as just another "cool meeting" were it not for Lady Trilby and her slightly feverish condition as she looked at the Pacific from her sickbed.

At first she was fascinated watching these young people in their short breeches, hurling their polished logs into the surf, paddling desperately toward the horizon, but finally she realized a tragedy was playing itself out in front of her very eyes. Her suspicion was confirmed when she opened her window slightly and summoned two young surfers about to plunge into the Pacific.

"You there, young men," she said.

The two boys stopped in their tracks and looked a little amused at Lady Trilby, in her red flannel nightrobe, a tasseled white knit cap securely on her head.

"What are you trying to do?"

"Get to Hawaii."

"Hawaii, why?"

"That's where the Big Ones are."

She was about to dissuade them, but they were already running to the sea with their boards, and she could do nothing but watch them and all the others hurl themselves against the pounding waves.

Well, grippe or no grippe, Lady Trilby knew that this called for action. She took the Service Manual from the shelf and studied it carefully then placed a long distance call to Whitehall. She reached Mr. Banks with little difficulty.

"Banks?"

"Yes."

"Ambassador Trilby here. Ramona."

"How are things?"

"Disastrous."

"Really? Is the revolution imminent?"

Lady Trilby could not catch the nuances over the transatlantic cable but cared little about them anyway.

"It's not a revolution," Lady Trilby said. "It's a mass exodus."

"A what?"

"I am watching it right from my window. Hundreds of men, hurling themselves against the waves on little logs trying to make their getaway."

"Where are they going?"

"Hawaii. I've asked them. They'll never make it. I've looked it up in the *Nautical Almanac,* it's twenty-three hundred miles due west. They'll all be drowned."

"Lady Trilby, I am rockbound; what do you expect me to do?"

"Send the British fleet to stand by. I've looked it up in the Service Manual. I have ambassadorial power to ask for naval support in an emergency."

"The fleet?"

"Yes, perhaps three capital ships."

"Three capital ships. I shall do my best."

"Your best is not too good, Mr. Banks. Do your utmost."

"Yes, Ambassador. Cheers."

"Cheers."

The phone call to England was only the first of the measures Lady Trilby instituted to meet the emergency. With the help of the Stoltz brothers she constructed a meager soup kitchen in front of the Embassy and festooned it with large prints of the ships *Cutty Sark,* the *Gloucester* and *Doubloon,* hoping somehow to teach these youngsters that oceans demand much of men and ships; and their desire to reach the "Big Ones" in Hawaii, whatever they were, could not be fulfilled with these little planks. But the surfers only smiled, took it all good-naturedly, partook of the warming soup and the nautical lectures, and then hurled themselves back into the ocean like lemmings.

Sunday dawned in Ramona Beach and with it the Finals of World Championship Surfing. It was a fine day, the sun rising hot and red in the east, its early rays warming the Pacific and its beaches. The contestants had risen with the sun, carefully polishing their boards for this day of days, testing the surf with practiced eyes and toes, noting the roll and dip of the waves, the undertow, the tidemarks, the spray and wind conditions.

Spectators by the thousands came to watch and enjoy the spectacle and a day in the sun. For miles and miles Ramona looked like a sea of bikinis, hundreds of surfboards stuck in the sand like a forest denuded of leaves, youngsters with guitars and bongos, men selling balloons, renting backrests, vendors hawking hot dogs, beer, photos of the surfing greats. A half-mile course of surf had been marked off for the competition, colorful pennants mounted on bamboo poles, each representing a great surfing area, and a judges' stand festooned with red, white and blue bunting rose in the center of the course. There sat the judges, past greats of the sport, a movie starlet, Mayor Taft, the Chamber of Commerce and, last but not least, Lady Trilby, who had been named Grand Marshal by the surfers for her kindness to them during the past week.

The events were divided into three categories, each involving various skills of the contestants. The first, a test for distance, proved the longest run a surfer could make on his board. The second consisted of "walking the board"—the participant walked from one end of the board to the other during his journey down the waves, the ultimate feat being to "hang ten," or stand perched on ten toes at the leading edge of the board. The last test was of acrobatics, and this event more than any other proved the skill and agility and inventiveness of the surfer.

All through it Lady Trilby stood on the reviewing stand in a flutter of anticipation. Repeatedly she scanned the horizon with her ancient spyglass, looking desperately for the British fleet to appear and stop the catastrophe.

And the fleet *did* appear. Her Majesty's Destroyer Escort *Thistle* slowly and majestically steamed past the grandstand of the Surfers' Convention almost at the conclusion of events and fired a brilliant, heartrending ten-gun salvo to the amazement, amusement and applause of the surfers, and the relief of Lady Trilby.

"There," Lady Trilby said proudly, "there goes a piece of England. Good show, boys. Perhaps this will teach them." She never knew what all this taught the surfers, since their convention had ended, but she watched with relief as they got out of the water, strapped their boards on their candy-colored conveyances and departed happily for other beaches, north, south, east or west.

Convinced that she had finally averted one tragedy in the colonies, Lady Trilby returned to her bed to finish out her grippe. As she placed a bit of myrrh in the vaporizer and inhaled that lovely English aroma, she wrote to Mr. Banks thanking him for the prompt intervention of the British fleet but reprimanding him for the error in protocol. "Ambassadors," she wrote, "rate a twelve-gun salvo. Not ten. Please remedy. Trilby."

13

Lady Trilby had slowly accustomed herself to the mores of the marriage of her boarders, though she instinctively sensed a certain tension in their relationship that worried her. Like a well-made symphony their voices seemed to sally from pianissimo to mezzoforte as the deadline of Pamela's weekly column drew near.

Both in their late twenties, they possessed a surfeit of physical and mental equipment to make a successful marriage. They were both from trouble-free familial backgrounds and both well educated. They had both dated and bedded amply and had approached marriage without the mysteries or taboos incumbent on previous generations. They understood progressive jazz and modern art, bullfighting, Danish furniture, Gide, Salinger and Heller. They loved skiing, surfing, sailing, cashmere sweaters and sports cars, Tanqueray Gin and old English pewter, and understood in depth the Volkswagen ads, the student non-violent movement and the pop value of Mandrake the Magician. They were a cool couple; they were "turned on." But coolness was hardly a state of mind which was easily attained. Living as they did in the cultural wastelands of Ramona Beach, it took a constant effort and alertness for them to keep up with their spiritual cousins on the East Coast, London, Paris, Nice, or wherever the action was at the moment.

This effort to keep up was more manifest with Pamela, whose profession demanded a constant working knowledge of the contemporary, much to the chagrin of her husband, whose nature was basically more introspective and even old-fashioned. He was continually bombarded with changing values. Of course, not all contemporary issues were Pamela's fault. Thomas' subscription to *Leisure Lad* was certainly a thorn in her side, as she saw a new rival pop up from the center of that magazine each month, *Leisure Lad,* after all, was the magazine touted for the solid state man who sleeps in a quilted circular bed.

"My only interest," Thomas would say, "is in the architecture of it all. There is nothing more beautiful in all of Nature than a naked young girl."

"That gives me an idea for a story, Thomas."

"Forget it, Pamela."

"Maybe one of those cool months, October, January. Just a little snow on my fanny."

"Pamela!"

"I think it would make one hell of a story, Thomas. Imagine, all our friends saying 'Hey, Pamela, haven't I seen you someplace before?' Fold into three parts, will you dear?"

"Look, Pamela," said Thomas, leveling a threatening forefinger in her direction, "if you have any idea of becoming a *Leisure Lad* pop-up—if you're even seriously entertaining the thought—I promise you—"

"I'm terribly sorry to interfere," said Lady Trilby, standing at the door, "but I'm in a bit of a dilemma."

"We were shouting again," Pamela apologized.

"Things are a bit tight here," Lady Trilby agreed, "but don't let me interfere. What is a *Leisure Lad* pop-up?"

Pamela smiled. "Show Lady Trilby, Thomas."

"Oh, for Christ sakes, Pamela."

"Show her."

"All right, all right." Thomas went to the bookcase, produced a copy of *Leisure Lad,* opened and unsprung a center spread on the coffee table.

"All right. July. In all her glory."

Lady Trilby opened her lorgnette, bent down and perused the naked little girl, studying each feature rather clinically, moving her glasses slowly up and down the undraped torso. Finally she tapped the page with her glasses and said, "Poor dear. With wrists like that she'd never be able to lift an iron kettle from the hearth."

"Let me see those wrists." Thomas now bent over the table and inspected the picture. "I'd never noticed."

"Thomas likes pictures of naked girls."

"Why, I should hope so," Lady Trilby said. "My late husband had a mistress who posed for the statue of Lady Godiva."

"Your husband had a mistress?" Pamela asked, a little shocked.

"Oh, he actually had several."

"Several?" Thomas now asked.

"Well, one at a time. He was a very faithful man really."

"And you knew all about it?"

"About what?"

"The mistresses?"

"Why of course. Don't you have a mistress, Thomas?"

"Me?"

"You, Thomas," Pamela spit out.

"No."

"Well, I think you are making a dreadful mistake."

"I am?"

"He is?"

"How does the saying go? 'Change was his mistress, chance his counselor.'" She looked at Pamela. "'Marriage is a boulevard, not a cul-de-sac.' That's Trilby. Isabella Trilby." She put her finger to her lips and returned to her parlor, but there was no need to admonish the Whites to be quiet, for her rather bohemian advice had thoroughly awed them.

"Would you like a mistress, Thomas?"

"One?"

"Several then."

"Several mistresses? I don't think *Leisure Lad* has ever discussed several mistresses."

"Tell me, Thomas, what did man do before *Leisure Lad* had a philosophy?"

"Groped in the darkness." Thomas shut the door and turned off the light and pursued his wife.

"Wait, Thomas, wait."

He pushed her on the couch, holding her arms, kissing her.

"Thomas."

"What, honey?"

"I just want to know whether we're on a dark boulevard or a cul-de-sac."

"It's all French to me. Come here."

Pamela White was a bright, headstrong columnist, but not a foolish one. She decided against becoming a *Leisure Lad* pop-up and abandoned the idea of being someone's mistress. A story was a story, no doubt, but if the job demanded the Perils of Pauline, it shouldn't have to embrace Gypsy Rose Lee. After all, other good columnists had succeeded still keeping their clothes on. There were enough problems in the world that would interest a mass audience.

She had heard of a local psychiatrist who was claiming a measure of success with a crash group-therapy session. He assembled the usual ten patients but rather than seeing them once or twice weekly over a period of years, he instructed all of them to wear clown suits and enter a large slow-moving centrifuge for forty-eight hours.

"This simulates the rotation of the earth," he explained to Pamela on her first interview, "the accelerated rate, of course, accentuates the fermentation of the problems. Like summer wheat. Pfffft—bing—bing—you know what I mean?"

"Pfffft—bing—bing?"

"That is the sound of fermenting summer wheat."

"I see," Pamela said, but she didn't see.

"We all don clown costumes before we enter the centrifuge. Symbolic, you know."

"Then you go along for the ride, Doctor?"

"Oh, heavens yes, would you like to see my costume?" He rose before Pamela could answer and continued in discourse as he walked to the closet in his office. "Actually the sessions would be more fruitful if we could orbit the centrifuge. Weightlessness is better than Miltown. How do you like my costume?"

"It's lovely."

"I like the ruffles at the collar, but the cleaners have a devil of a time starching them."

"Tell me about the weightlessness, Doctor."

He settled in his chair again and lit his water pipe. "It is my theory that we've all been traumatized by gravity."

"Really?"

"Do you remember dropping things as a child?"

"I suppose I did, but I don't remember," Pamela said.

"You *do* remember, you repress. Toys, plates, glasses,

jars of martini onions. It's a terribly frustrating experience."

"I suppose it is," Pamela said, dropping her pencil.

"Now then, what magazine did you say you worked for?"

"*Panorama.*"

"*Panorama,* yes. That has a large circulation doesn't it?"

"Five million panting readers."

"Five million panting readers. Well, are you going to join one of our sessions? There is an opening next weekend."

"Why not. You're sure—" Pamela hesitated.

"Sure of what?"

"Well, it won't do anything to me."

"Like what?"

"Well, I'm fairly normal. You know. Like apple pie."

"Well," the doctor said, "apples can be troublesome fruit, you know."

Pamela laughed slightly. "All right, Doctor. I'll be there. All ears."

"Good. Countdown at three-fifty. We start spinning at four P.M. on Friday."

14

· · · · · · · · ·

There were not many licensed architects in Ramona Beach, so it is not too surprising that the Gutter brothers selected Thomas White's name from the directory. One morning they appeared in his drafting room, carrying a large map which they quickly spread out on the drafting table.

"You're a bona fide architect, aren't you, kid?" asked Walter, but Thomas' youthfulness had prompted that question before, and he took no offense.

"Here's the plan," Willie said, pacing the room and stabbing at the map. "We're going to level this area here."

"Level it?" Thomas looked a little shocked.

"Yeah, level it. And then we're going to put up a retirement community."

"For old folks," Walter said.

"Old folks, young folks, who cares. The government will finance anybody over forty-two."

"Forty-two?" Thomas asked. "For retirement?"

"How old are you, kid?"

"Twenty-nine."

"Well, in a few years you'll be over the hill. Anyway, here's what we need. First of all a good name for the development."

"How about Over the Hill?" Thomas suggested.

"That's not bad, kid, not bad at all. We need about five hundred units, one bedrooms, two bedrooms, the usual junk, you know, hobby shop, card room, lawn bowling, bird walks, a bingo parlor."

Thomas said nothing.

"Now I want you to design this in contemporary Moorish. That's *big* right now. Beaded curtains, bedrooms facing east, tin lanterns, lots of adobe, straw roofs, anyways, you know what I mean."

Thomas knew what they meant.

"You want me to build five hundred adobe huts with straw roofs."

"No. We want you to build a model hut, now you got me doing it, a model *apartment* and the funeral parlor. That's the most important part of the development."

"A funeral parlor?"

"Yeah. What's the matter, kid, you a little deaf?"

"You're going to put a funeral parlor right in the middle of the development?"

"Sure, that's all these folks got on their mind. They're not buying a pig in a poke."

Thomas finally had enough. "I'm quite backlogged," he said. "I'm doing the design for the Gordon guillotine, you know."

"What's that?"

"It's a kit," Thomas continued, now stuck with the fabrication. "Thirty-nine ninety-five. You can build your own guillotine. A child can assemble it. Good sturdy oak frame and six injector stainless steel blades. Really works. Great Christmas item."

"Well, if you're too busy, kid. . . ."

"I don't see how you're going to get permission to level that whole area."

"You let us worry about *that*. The Mayor and us are like that!"

"I am not interested, gentlemen," Thomas said. "It's bad enough herding all the young people into apartments, but the thought of funneling older people into these stucco slums is too depressing."

"You'll make a fortune," Walter Gutter said. "You get a royalty on every hut that's sold."

"I said I'm not interested." Thomas stood up.

"Well, if you don't need the money, we'll find someone who does."

They left Thomas, and he sat at his drafting table, his head between his hands. He *did* need the money. Where the hell was Pamela? Why wasn't she at his side at trying times like these? But he knew she couldn't be, not while she was working for *Panorama,* off on some assignment now; he remembered her saying something about that analyst fellow. He picked up his pencil and found himself unconsciously making drawings (and good ones) of Gordon guillotines.

Pamela's return Sunday afternoon rather than relieving his misery only heightened it. She did not walk into the house, she reeled in, flailing her arms wildly, wearing the most absurd clown suit, shouting at the top of her lungs, "Where is that lousy father figure? I'll kill him."

"Pamela."

"There you are. Stand still, Thomas."

"I am standing still."

"You are not, Thomas, you're spinning, everything is

spinning. You, you, you *superego*, yes sir, you *super-ego*."

"Pamela."

"Don't touch me. Don't touch me, Thomas, and stop spinning. You think you've got troubles, why one of the men in our session never had a mother at all, and he could prove it."

"Really?"

"Yes. He could prove it. Where you and I have a navel he had a Nixon button."

"Pamela, honey, please sit down. Lie down, any-thing—"

"Oh, no you don't, Thomas. I know what you have in mind. I know what's under those curly locks."

"What?"

"Goulash. Hungarian goulash. Forty-eight hours of Hungarian goulash. Morning, noon and night—but I'm free, emancipated. *Stop spinning.*"

Thomas finally succeeded in putting Pamela on the bed, but he could not, try as he would, remove her clown outfit.

"Well, well, what have we here?" asked Lady Trilby as she watched the poor girl hold on to a corner of their four-poster bed.

"She's either drunk or she's mad," Thomas said.

Lady Trilby sat next to Pamela and tried to feel her forehead.

"Don't you touch me," Pamela yelled. "All you foreigners are Jungians. I know the kind."

Lady Trilby rose and motioned Thomas to join her in the hallway. "She's quite mad," she said.

"I know. What should I do?"

"Well, if I were a man, I'd hit her. Hard. You do that and I'll fetch a doctor. I know just the man." She ran downstairs to rouse her neighbor.

"We've got to get some help to the poor girl, Captain Sabella," Lady Trilby pleaded. "Isn't Alfonse's brother a head doctor?"

"Yes. But he is away."

"Well, then, fetch Alfonse. He's had at least *some* experience."

"But his brother is wearing the suit."

"Well lend him one of yours. I don't think the girl would know the difference."

And so Alfonse came and his treatment bore out the contention of many good medical practitioners that kindness and warmth are still the greatest form of therapy extant. Of course, the poor man was somewhat reluctant at first. He was not accustomed to making house calls nor versed in healing hysterical patients. He tried his weekly habit of sitting behind the patient, hands meekly folded on his lap, nodding his head, but he soon realized that he could not reach the poor girl, and came to the awful realization that he would have to *say* something. He spoke softly.

"What do you know about fish?" he asked.

"Fish?"

"Yes. Sailfish, bonita, yellowtail, fried fish, boiled, marinated."

"Oh?"

"Do you like fish, Pamela?"

"Oh, yes, Doctor."

"I like fish too. What's your favorite fish, Pamela?"

"Goldfish."

"Mine too. And guppies."

"Yes, guppies. Tiny little guppies. And kingfish," Pamela said.

"And Amos and Andy."

"Yes, and fish and chips."

"And three little fishes." And then Pamela fell asleep.

"I don't know how to thank you, Doctor," Thomas said, but Alfonse was very modest about his success.

"Is there anything I should do in case she wakes up?"

"Take her to a restaurant and buy her a good fish dinner."

"A good fish dinner," Thomas said to himself, walking slowly toward Lady Trilby's kitchen after he said farewell to Alfonse.

"Is that you, Thomas?"

"Yes."

"How's Pamela?"

"Asleep."

"Good. Jolly good. Come have a spot of brandy. You look a bit shaky."

"I am," he confessed.

She filled two glasses and seated herself across from him. "Now then, Thomas, things seem a bit sticky with you and Pamela."

"That's putting it mildly." Thomas took a long hard sip of his brandy and propped his feet on a kitchen stool.

"It all seemed rather idyllic at the beginning. Pam worked, I worked. We decided not to have any children until we had earned enough to buy a home, furnish it. A decent car, a little in the savings account, a trip to Europe, you know. And Pamela *really* is quite successful. Her column is popular, she is making headway, but the cost of that job to our marriage is prohibitive."

"Well then, forbid her to work."

"I am trying desperately to retain a vestige of integrity in my profession. Yesterday a couple of developers approached me. They offered me a commission."

"That's wonderful, Thomas."

"It wasn't wonderful. They wanted me to design a contemporary Moorish retirement community."

"What in heaven's name is that?"

"It is a housing development for older retired people. No children, shuffleboard, square dancing, chess, hobby shops."

"No children! My word. Shuffleboard! Good Lord."

"They've been rather successful," Thomas continued. "Perhaps it's as good a way to put that generation out to pasture as any."

"What ages are these old folks, Thomas?"

"You have to be forty-two to qualify."

"Forty-*two!* Retire at forty-two! No wonder you're discouraged."

Lady Trilby stood and paced the kitchen floor. "Pagan rites, pagan rites," she mumbled. "I've seen these symptoms before. In Cyprus we had the same problem. The natives would sit around all day waiting for one of their own to die. Funerals were great fun, all ritual and tears and wine and sentiment."

"I'm not so sure how much sentiment is involved here. The developers want to level a whole section of Ramona Beach. This very block is destined for oblivion."

"But there are laws. You can't just take people's dwellings."

"Laws can be changed, Lady Trilby. The Gutter brothers stated that they had the Mayor in their back pockets."

"Well, this is nasty business, Thomas. Nasty business. I can see your dilemma. Can't you do something else? Don't you have another talent?"

"I'm afraid not."

"Let me ponder the situation a bit; I must get off my dispatches."

Thomas returned to his studio a little perplexed, and Lady Trilby put a rose on Queen Victoria's photograph. It would have been her birthday.

15

· · · · · · · ·

Lady Trilby assumed that the explosive nature of the last meeting of the Afternoon Society had ended her relationship with the A.G.A.I.N.S.T. women, but she was wrong. They may have been dented a bit, bruised perhaps, but no one should underestimate the stamina of those patriots. After months of secret conclaving, they finally went to City Hall and assembled in Mayor Taft's office to enlist his help in ridding Ramona Beach of this terribly dangerous woman.

"There were spies floating by the window," one woman explained hysterically.

"Spies?" Mayor Taft asked.

"Yes, she called one of them Captain."

"I see."

"And they were *floating* by the window."

"One up, and one down."

"And she is holding prisoners," another woman screamed.

"We saw them trying to escape when the bomb went off."

"Prisoners? A bomb?"

"You don't believe us, do you?"

"No," Mayor Taft admitted.

"Well, go there yourself."

"I can't."

"Why not?"

"We've already tried to do something. It's a British Embassy. It's foreign soil."

"There must be something you can do. After all, you're the Mayor."

"Do you like being Mayor?" one woman asked.

"Why do you ask?"

"Because if you don't do something about Lady Trilby, A.G.A.I.N.S.T. may decide on their own candidate for Mayor."

"Well, ladies," Mayor Taft stammered, "I think that if you have access to the Embassy, then by all means you should maintain the contact."

"You mean go back there?"

"Precisely."

"We might all get killed."

"Well, leave some reserves at home."

"I think the Mayor has a point," one elderly lady said.

"Sure, but he's only telling us to risk our lives. What about him?"

"I shall do my utmost, ladies, my very utmost." He reached into a desk drawer. "Have some bumper stickers. They've just been delivered from the printer's." He opened the package and handed out the paper strips. They read

VOTE FOR TAFT
FROM THE GUTTERS

"Well, Mr. Mayor, what's this?" one woman said, showing them to His Honor.

"Oh, my goodness. Let me have those. There must be some mistake."

"No," the ladies said. "We'll hold on to them. You perform and we won't have to affix them to our cars. Fair enough?"

Unlike other ultraconservative organizations, A.G.A.I.N.S.T. did not believe in burning crosses on the lawns. They burned down the house and left the landscaping intact. Secret orders were issued to burn the Embassy to the ground, but nothing was to be mentioned to Mayor Taft. One could never trust a politician, even if he professed to be on the side of the angels.

Mayor Taft *did* explore every avenue available to make life difficult for Lady Trilby, but diplomatic immunity checked him at every move. Then after much investigation he discovered that Lady Trilby was flying two unlicensed pigeons. He phoned the Animal Bureau and discovered to his chagrin that they did not at the moment have pigeon licenses in stock.

"Well, hang a dog license around their necks. We need the revenue. Besides, you can't have unlicensed pigeons flying around," he shouted into the receiver and hung up.

And so two burly officials arrived at the Embassy to license Lady Trilby's birds. One had a bushy mustache, and inadvertently reminded Lady Trilby of the false Englishman whom the Whites had described months before.

"What foul deed is this? These birds are in Her Majesty's Service," Lady Trilby protested.

"If it's an animal, it's got to be licensed," said the inspector.

"By whose authority?"

"It's the law, lady. Come on, where are the birds? We haven't got all day."

"One bird is on a mission. It won't be back for a month."

"A month?"

"Yes. It takes two weeks for the bird to return from England and then it's going on a two-week holiday."

"The bird?"

"Of course. Don't you get a holiday?"

"Yeah, sure." The two men looked at each other, but the mustached one prodded his partner. "Come on, let's hang the license on the other bird and get out of here."

"Yeah, we'll just license one bird today."

"And if I refuse?"

"We'll shoot him."

"In cold blood?"

"I always thought birds had cold blood anyway."

"I fail to see your humor, but I suppose I must protect my underlings."

She led them to the cage and watched the men hang a three-ounce brass license on a four-ounce pigeon.

"How do you expect that poor bird to fly with that huge brass sign about his neck?"

The two men stood back and surveyed the poor pigeon, already quite weary from the weight.

"Well," the mustached one said somewhat sheepishly, "maybe the other one will be more robust from its holiday. Come on, Red, let's get outta here."

The two were almost out the front door when Lady Trilby barred their way with her walking stick. With a deft flick of the wrist, she tapped her cane against their ankles and the mustached inspector fell to the floor.

"What do you say now, impostor?" Lady Trilby said, towering over the fallen man.

"Impostor?"

"How are things in Piccadilly?"

Before he could answer, the redhead bent down and helped his compatriot to his feet and the two bolted to the street, arm in arm.

"I swear," the mustached one said, "we ought to hang a license on her."

But the license about the pigeon's neck was the straw that broke the camel's back. That evening Lady Trilby informed Whitehall that her days of contemplation were over.

Messrs. Warner and Banks
The Foreign Office, Whitehall

Gentlemen:

I cannot, I admit, judge this entire nation from my lonely outpost, but I must assume that I am acquainted with a fairly representative selection of the populace, and before going into detail I shall state, categorically, that the loss of this colony is no loss at all. As I have reported in previous communiqués, I am forever dismayed to see the natives endlessly lounge about in the sun. Even you will admit I have taken a somewhat charitable viewpoint about this and attributed it to malnutrition and the importune climate. But conversations with my boarders have convinced me that America is a lost cause. A whole section of this town is to be leveled and replaced by a Moorish retirement community, and imagine—the retirement age of the natives is forty-two! I can only say that any people that rises from the beaches only to enter a retirement community is hardly worth fighting for.

This lethargy is, of course, producing serious social effects. Only the opportune arrival of the Destroyer Escort *Thistle* prevented the mass exodus which I feared; more recently one of my boarders, a lovely young girl, went stark raving mad.

Nevertheless, I shall await your reply before applying for a transfer. Trilbys are historically not quitters, but neither are they fools. Service, after all, is measured by the served.

I almost succeeded today in apprehending that dangerous mustached impostor. Had him bloody well down, all right, but he managed to escape. He came to molest Operator 111, but I have heard he's been lurking about the Embassy before. I strongly urge you to send one of our best counterespionage agents to clean out this menace.

Awaiting your agent and orders,

Respectfully,
Trilby

Pigeon follows with details.

16

Lady Trilby's slightly myopic condition may well excuse her suspicion of every mustached man in her vicinity, but her trepidations about a bogus Englishman snooping around the property were very well founded. For the bogus Englishman the Whites had mentioned *was* indeed bogus, and his presence represented an espionage blunder which was corrected much too late.

One must admit, however, that British activities in Ramona Beach certainly appeared peculiar, and eyebrows were raised in certain international circles. Why, asked hostile foreign powers, did England feel it necessary to send a full-fledged ambassador to a sleepy community where a vice-consul would certainly suffice?

Red China, perhaps the most paranoid nation at the opposite end of the Pacific, decided to dispatch their best man, the Red Canary, the most dreaded spy of the Orient.

One wonders how a young boy, raised in a rural canton of Peking, dared rival the great masters of espionage like Mata Hari or McLean of England, but like many great careers, his was shaped not so much by talent as by affliction. Though a future in his father's rice paddies was assured at birth, a combination of hay fever and chronic athlete's foot prevented him from toiling the ancestral fields, surrounded as they were by pollen and buried, of necessity, under a foot of water. Therefore, he had to look elsewhere for a livelihood. One day a traveling theater group visited his district, and the classic actors in their rich costumes made a lasting impression on the already sensitive boy. Night after night, sneezing and scratching his toes, he begged his family to give him permission to join the troupe. They finally capitulated. After years of apprenticeship with the theater company he emerged a star. He had mastered the art of acting, make-up, costume, even sleight of hand; he had studied foreign languages and mimicry. His pantomime imitation of Japanese Emperor Hirohito on a zoological mission became a national sensation. Hardly a Chinese citizen alive will ever forget the image of the Red Canary dressed in a cutaway chasing a mythical butterfly.

But unfortunately the Chinese had domestic problems and these touched the lives of most citizens: Chiang Kai-shek moved to Formosa (to be closer to the China Lobby in Washington) and most of the day he stood on a hillside waving a small paper flag, while his wife was busy lecturing to freshly scrubbed girls at Ivy League colleges because of her weakness for the chicken pot pie invariably served at luncheons. Mao Tse-tung immersed himself in water to prove his eternal youth, and the Red Canary was told by the local People's Committee that his acting career must come to an end. His talents were needed in the espionage office of his government.

Though he missed performing on the stage, spying had certain compensations: It gave him an opportunity to travel, enabled him to use all his acting talents, and afforded him a chance to be a patriot. His mother often said he was a regular Chinese Ronald Reagan.

And so the Red Canary found himself aboard the *Nippon Flower* bound from Peking to Ramona to begin his fortieth mission.

For an ex-actor half the fun of espionage was the costumes. As his journey ended, he rummaged through his espionage kit and decided to masquerade as a Royal Mounted Policeman. He liked the look of the scarlet coat and black breeches, and he walked on deck to test his disguise. Unfortunately the first fellow passenger he encountered, a rather dowdy lady botanist, said, "My, don't you look nice. Getting ready for the Captain's ball?" Perplexed, the Red Canary returned to his cabin and changed to a gypsy costume. Though he looked less dashing and found it awkward to attach the gold ring to his ear lobe, he had to admit that he was definitely more disguised. Once more he revisited the deck, only to encounter the same lady botanist.

"I shouldn't wear *that*," she said, "the Mountie costume is much more becoming."

Foiled again, the Red Canary entered the ship's bar disconsolately, and ordered a double rye.

"My, my," the Japanese bartender said, "don't we look pretty with the gold ring through the ear."

"It's not a gold ring," the Red Canary said.

"It's not, what is it?"

"It's radar."

"I see," the bartender said, "and how do you feel about the Green Bay Packers?"

The next morning the *Nippon Flower* made port in San Pedro, the Red Canary debarked inconspicuously and checked into a local waterfront hotel. But he soon made his first mistake. Since he would be dealing primarily with an Englishwoman, he decided to pose as one of her countrymen and donned a bowler hat, a good mustache, houndstooth checked jacket, jodhpurs, polished cordovan boots. He made up his cheeks to look ruddy and painted fine reddish-blue lines about his cheeks and nose. He slid corn-blue contact lenses over his brown eyes and armed himself with a good umbrella. However, after weeks of scouting the Embassy and the beaches, he realized that in a casual, near naked, denimed, bermudaed, capried society like Ramona Beach, he stuck out like the proverbial sore thumb and was well observed. Even by the Whites. A change in costume was in order. He spent one afternoon rifling his steamer trunk and after many changes finally decided to dress as a girl scout leader.

Proudly he stood in front of the narrow mirror in his room tugging at his wig, admiring the proper patches on his sleeve, and finally he dared into the street and felt quite secure as two young boy scouts helped him cross the street.

He proceeded to the Embassy at once and boldly

knocked on the door. Lady Trilby answered herself.

"I'm Mrs. Pennybaker," the Red Canary said. "We're conducting our annual girl scout cooky drive."

"Ah, sweet charity, sweet charity. Come in, come in."

As he entered the Embassy, his well-trained eyes made mental notes of all he beheld.

"Would you like some tea?" Lady Trilby asked.

"I wouldn't mind," the Red Canary said, "if you will buy some cookies."

"Yes, yes, of course, how much are they?"

"They're fifty cents a box and send a little girl to camp."

"Well, isn't that jolly. I shall take three boxes, then the girl will have some company."

The Red Canary had bought the cookies in good faith from a merchant in San Pedro and was unaware that the boxes did not contain cookies but stale bagels. Lady Trilby made the discovery at once. Perhaps another day she would not have been quite so suspicious, but with the impending revolution and strangers stirring about the place, she dared not take any chances.

She phoned the police and told them that a lady was on her premises selling unofficial girl scout cookies. They were quite pleasant and promised to dispatch officers to the scene immediately.

Trying to stall, she asked the Red Canary to join her in the hallway. She picked up a flag and took a heroic stance in front of an ancient full length mirror.

"How do you think I look?" she asked.

"Pardon me, madame?"

"I mean, do I look like a proper statue?"

"Oh, no, madame."

"I don't? What do I look like?" Lady Trilby seemed somewhat offended.

"I mean only that you are too much a woman for me to envision you as a statue."

"Well, you *must*. I expect some reward from the natives."

"I see," said the Red Canary, and he suddenly found his hands clasped by a pair of handcuffs.

"What's this?" he protested, looking into the stern eyes of the local constabulary.

"You're under arrest, lady."

"I'm not a lady," the Red Canary protested.

"You're telling me," the officer said. "Imagine, passing off stale bagels for girl scout cookies."

They led him away, booked him and jailed him. But of course the Red Canary found it simple to escape from the local jail. During the long night he managed to change his costume, and during the morning line-up he posed as the local health officer and placed the entire prison under quarantine. But he knew he was no closer to the truth about the affairs of Lady Trilby.

His problems were also financial. Since he was an agent of an impoverished, oil-poor nation, his stipend was quite inadequate for so freewheeling a high-income neighborhood as Ramona Beach, and he found it necessary to get a part-time position to keep body and soul together. He managed this by taking a position as a driver for the Good Humor Company. This afforded him both a certain degree of mobility, helpful in his espionage activities, and allowed him to be around children, which he genuinely liked.

But the Red Canary knew all too well his job in

Ramona Beach was not to sell ice cream to youngsters nor to sit idly on the beach and enjoy the sight of nymphets entering and exiting the Pacific surf. He was here to assess and contain a danger to his government, and he never lost sight of this. He closely watched the Embassy and the movements of Lady Trilby. Even her exploits in her little golf cart were observed. But he could not determine anything conspiratorial about her activities, and only the comings and goings of the carrier pigeons distinguished her residence from the houses of her neighbors.

With the assistance of a local ornithologist he obtained the proper lure (a Burmese worm) that would halt the pigeons long enough to allow him to read the messages carried in small capsules on their legs. The worms proved effective, but the pigeon messages made little sense to him except to show him that he was regarded as a suspicious character. He finally decided to abandon his endless array of disguises and get to the source of his quest. A particularly succulent Burmese worm arrested Operator 111 on his return from Whitehall, and the Red Canary substituted the message he was carrying with one of his own which read: "SENDING SECRET AGENT TO YOUR EMBASSY TO HELP YOU WITH COUNTERESPIONAGE. HIS PASSWORD SHALL BE 'MOTHERHOOD.' EXTEND HIM USUAL DIPLOMATIC COURTESIES—BANKS."

He chose the following Thursday, his day off from the Good Humor Company, as the time to arrive at the enemy's citadel.

That afternoon the ladies from A.G.A.I.N.S.T. once more assembled in the Trilby parlor and played the game with the Ambassador. There was the usual record, a short lecture by Lady Trilby on the nutritional value of old-fashioned oatmeal and finally the usual offer of tea, which they accepted.

When Lady Trilby had gone to the kitchen, they busied themselves by searching the premises for damaging evidence, but their hostess kept a spartan, orderly house and outside of the *Hotel Red Book* they had to settle for an advertisement for the Gordon guillotine, which any child could put together for $39.95. Lady Trilby waltzed innocently into her parlor carrying a tray full of teacups and a plate heaped with sugar cookies and hardly noticed as one of the women slipped the damaging drawing into her purse.

"Now then," she asked, "who will have lemon and who will have sugar?"

"A little of both," said a short, bearded man, stepping through the open window.

Lady Trilby, herself quite startled, looked with amazement at the stranger, who wore a slightly soiled mandarin cap, tails, weskit, striped pants and paper sandals.

"Well, ladies," the stranger said, "what have we here? A lecture on motherhood?"

"Motherhood? Oh, *motherhood*," said Lady Trilby as she put down her cup and extended her hand. "You must be from the Secret Service."

"Please," the man said, "not so loud."

"I mean from Whitehall," Lady Trilby corrected herself.

"Yes, Whitehall."

"Well," Lady Trilby said, "tapping the bottom of her cup for attention, "I should like you to meet a real secret agent."

"An agent?"

"Secret agent," the bearded man corrected, now quite adamant.

"Secret agent?"

"Didn't you see me come through the window? Where's my tea?"

"Yes, the tea." Lady Trilby poured and passed, and its consumption brought a minute of quiet to the Embassy until one of the ladies let out a horrible scream as she fished a gray eyeball out of her teacup. And so the meeting ended.

When the A.G.A.I.N.S.T. ladies had left, perhaps for the last time, Lady Trilby set about to make things comfortable for the secret agent.

"You shall have this room," she said, showing him the quarters vacated by the Stoltz brothers.

The agent looked about the room and was satisfied except for the window.

"Why is the window barred?"

"It's not barred," Lady Trilby said.

"What do you call this?" He walked to the iron bars against the window.

"There used to be an elevator in here," she said. "I had it taken out."

"There was an elevator in here?"

"Yes, rather a historic one. Foch used it to sign the Versailles Treaty."

"Of course."

"We're all a bit tight here," Lady Trilby said, "so I shall ask you to observe a few simple rules."

"Rules?"

"Yes. One of my boarders is a pretty young matron who has delusions that everything is spinning."

"Everything is spinning."

"Yes, she thinks the whole earth goes round, you know the sort of thing."

"The earth goes round." The secret agent found himself repeating each of Lady Trilby's statements like an idiot.

"The doctor has instructed us to agree with her to speed her recovery."

"Agree with her that the earth is going round."

"Precisely."

"Well, that shouldn't be difficult."

"No. I serve three solid meals a day, high tea at four and bouillon at ten. And I do not tolerate the harp. You don't play the harp?"

"As a matter of fact—"

"Yes?"

"I don't."

"Well then, we shall get along." Lady Trilby left the gaping agent standing in the middle of the room, but returned almost immediately.

"I forgot one thing."

"Yes?"

"We both know you are a secret agent."

He nodded his head. "You saw me come through the window."

"Well, I am trying to teach the natives manners and I have nothing against espionage just so long as one isn't underhanded about it."

"I couldn't agree with you more, dear lady."

"So I have had this little button made for you and I would appreciate your wearing it when you're working." She gave him a plastic button perhaps two inches in diameter. It was white with red letters spelling out "I SPY." "See you at supper. Cheerio." She went to the kitchen, made herself some tea and ate a stale bagel.

17
· · · · · · · ·

To suggest to Captain Sabella that helium, hydrogen or coal gas would serve very well as a propellant for his balloon would be like pointing out to a Vermont farmer the superiority of steam heat to the crackling logs of an open fireplace. There were few enough unadulterated pleasures left to a man these days and the Captain meant to savor one of those few remaining. Consequently, his balloon was of the earliest design known, modeled after the craft used by the Montgolfier brothers in 1783. The only change wrought by two hundred years of civilization was that Captain Sabella used a barbecue pit rather than a pile of burning straw on the floor of his wicker basket to heat the air going into the bag. He reasoned that should he ever be lucky enough to ascend to a height which would afford him some leisure, he could use this locomotive brazier to broil a good steak. Other than that minor improvement, the balloon was a perfect reproduction of the early model. There was a mystery, however: He was never able to ascend more than thirty-five feet whereas the Montgolfiers had easily soared to five hundred feet.

Two things troubled Captain Sabella: his inability to rise sufficiently; and the explosions which inevitably brought him down. Since he used no explosive gases to propel his craft, why should it explode? Time and time again he checked and rechecked the drawings from which his balloon had been built, and time and time again he rebuilt it literally from scratch, and time and time again the balloon exploded.

He had even begged the Stoltz brothers, even *one* Stoltz brother, to accompany him on a journey to point out an error in handling of which he might be unaware, but the sight of the Captain repeatedly plummeting to earth in his wicker basket, even from such a humble altitude as thirty-five feet, took all the courage out of their hearts. His invitations invariably prompted them to a litany of aeronautical disasters from Icarus to the *Hindenburg*. "Man has no right to go any higher than an elevator can take him. It is not civilized," they argued. Jeder Mensch sein eigenes Himmelreich, Sabella thought, and let it go at that.

Yet for all the misgivings the brothers had about ballooning, they deeply respected Sabella's devotion to the art and gave unstintingly of their time and energy to try to find the cause of the Captain's continued misfortunes. But the conferences held around the Captain's Franklin stove proved unfruitful.

It was not until the day they topped out the shaft of their five-story elevator that they suspected the cause of Sabella's problems. It was true that the Captain's balloon was a perfect replica of the early model, and equally true that the heat generated by the barbecue would lighten the air inside the balloon as efficiently as the straw burned by the Montgolfiers. The only other change made by the Captain was a personal one, and it was precisely this which caused the disasters.

Any method of heating air, whether it is a brazier or straw, burning coal or logs, is bound to produce sparks. Since all of the materials in a balloon are flammable, it is, of course, necessary for the pilot to carry liquids aloft with which to douse the infant blazes. The Montgolfiers carried water. Captain Sabella carried wine.

Being basically a bassoonist, not a balloonist, he admitted to a few apprehensions whenever he stepped into his straw gondola, but once inside, warmed by the brazier, looking at the huge colored sphere looming over his head like the awning of a four-poster bed, he felt quite safe. He stirred the coals, let go the guy ropes and ascended.

The Stoltz brothers, sitting on their lofty perch, carefully watched all these proceedings for the twentieth time in hopes of detecting the crucial error which would ultimately defeat their comrade, and this day their vigil was rewarded. The stirring of the brazier after departure had caused some sparks and a small fire was starting on the underside of the balloon. Sabella, still ascending, calmly took off his bandanna, soaked it in wine and doused the flames. The explosion ensued. The Stoltz brothers, dodging the falling shreds of the balloon said almost in unison, "The wine, it's the wine."

But their discovery of the source of the Captain's failures did not immediately suggest a way of imparting this information tactfully. It was not proper to accept a man's hospitality on one hand and insult his wine on the other, but once more fate played into their hands.

That very same evening the Captain asked them to join him for dinner, and as the night wore on, the Stoltzes stood about and toasted Captain's Sabella's courageous spirit. Then with much aplomb they threw their not quite empty glasses into the Franklin stove. The ensuing explosion almost caused the third rupture of the day. The first, the balloon; the second, the Franklin stove; and the third, the friendship of Ambassador Trilby, who stood in the doorway, candle, nightcap and blunderbuss, saying, somewhat officiously, "If you must pop your blimp, Captain, I would appreciate it if you would do it outdoors. *Good night!*"

"Of course," Sabella said, scarcely noticing her. "It's that goddamned Genoese wine."

"Well, it may well be the Genoese wine, Captain, but admission of one's weakness is only the first step to restitution."

"I could not agree with you more, dear lady. Come boys, come, let's mend that damned balloon. Samoa, here I come!"

18
· · · · · · · ·

It was receipt of the first condemnation notice that finally stirred Lady Trilby into direct political action.

"Will you look at this," she said to Thomas, pointing to the letter, "the right of eminent domain, it's laughable."

"It may be for you, Lady Trilby. They probably won't be able to touch the Embassy, but it's not very amusing for all your neighbors who are at the mercy of the city."

"The mercy of the city." Lady Trilby tapped the edge of the kitchen table. "You mean the Lord Mayor."

"Yes," Thomas admitted, "he is the elected head."

"Elected by whom?"

"The people."

"Well, why don't they elect someone else? If the man threatens their homes, why should they retain him in office?"

"Old Mayor Taft has a pretty good machine. He's been in power a long time."

"How are things going on with you and Pamela, Thomas?" she asked abruptly.

The question caught him rather nakedly, and he betrayed his troubles more openly than he was wont to.

"I think we're heading for trouble."

"She's not seeing that doctor any more?"

"Which one, the fish doctor or the turning doctor?"

"The turning one."

"No, no, that's all taken care of. But Pamela has a new idea for a story. Free-falling."

"What is that?"

"You throw yourself out of an airplane and plunge to earth."

"In England we used to call that suicide."

"I'd call it suicide too, but Pamela insists it would make a good story; she even wants me to try it."

"Are you going to oblige?"

"Hell no. Pamela insists that I refuse because my mother wouldn't let me collect butterflies."

Lady Trilby shook her head.

"I should like to ask three more personal questions, Thomas."

"Go ahead."

"Have you ever been in jail; are you of legitimate birth; and are you now or have you ever been a Communist agent?"

"You must be kidding."

"Hardly; just answer me."

"The answer is no."

"You mean you've never been incarcerated or a Communist, but you are a proper bastard?"

"I beg your pardon." Thomas seemed genuinely offended.

"It is a respectable generic word you know."

"I mean yes, no," Thomas stammered. "I'm not a bastard."

"I'll second that," said Pamela, slipping an arm about her husband's neck as she joined them in the kitchen.

"What is that *thing* you're wearing?" Lady Trilby said, rather sharply.

"A muumuu. Why?"

"Well, young lady, we'd better get you some more respectable clothes."

"What's wrong with muumuus?"

"They're hardly appropriate for the wife of a candidate for Lord Mayor!"

"Lord Mayor? Who's running for Lord Mayor?"

"Thomas," she said, kicking him rather severely under the table.

"Thomas, for Lord Mayor? That's very funny."

Thomas, rubbing his injured shin, was not amused by Lady Trilby's kick nor Pamela's reaction, and that anguished moment may well be recorded in history as the birth of a new statesman.

"Being neither a convict, a Commie nor a bastard," he said in injured tones, "I've decided to cast my lot with the people of Ramona Beach, and stamp out poverty, rid the community of pestilence, put the three R's back into education and send the Gutters back where they came from."

"Hear, hear," Lady Trilby said, standing now, "such a good resonant voice, I think I'll raise the standard early. It's such a banner day."

"You're really serious, aren't you, Thomas?"

"Of course."

"But why?"

"I'll tell you why, Pamela. For years now I've been thinking about capitalizing on the legitimacy of my birth, but I never felt it was enough. Last night you finally hit on the real reason for my hesitancy."

"I did? Last night? What reason?"

"I think all of this started when my mother wouldn't let me collect butterflies."

The following day Lady Trilby had assembled everyone—Captain Sabella, the Stoltz brothers, Pamela, friends of the Whites—to inaugurate the campaign.

"We've got to collect a crowd. We must get Thomas' name before the voters."

"And how do you propose to do that?"

"Announce a public hanging," Lady Trilby said.

"A public hanging?" Thomas stuttered.

"Yes, let's get some handbills printed. State the name and location of the event, build a scaffolding and we'll collect a mob in a jiffy."

"Wait a minute. Whom are you going to hang?"

"I should think the present Lord Mayor."

"No, no, Lady Trilby," Thomas said, rather fatherly, "that's not the way it works in a democracy."

"You, you Thomas White, candidate for Lord Mayor, presume to tell *me*, Lady Trilby, about democracy?"

"When it comes to you, Lady Trilby," Thomas said quite respectfully, "presumption goes out the window."

Captain Sabella was not the only man in our fair land interested in ascension. Since the days of Icarus, the envelope of air surrounding our planet has challenged men and nations; for some it has been merely high adventure, for others an object of conquest; the skies have brought out the very best and very worst in humanity. But NASA certainly is the most outrageous example of a rich nation grossly abusing the elements.

No one in his right mind—and this includes much of

the eminent personnel working for the space agency—has any desire to go to the moon. It is, it must be admitted, an unfortunate piece of real estate, like Baltimore, Oakland, Frankfurt or even Detroit on a Sunday. It has no charm, no beauty and, in these days of H bombs and missile silos, certainly no military value. Unfortunately, the advent of free public education in the United States has spawned a new breed of individuals who are obsessed with mathematics, and there can be, after all, just so many checkers in supermarkets. A responsible nation has to employ its citizens. A moonshot is the answer. It can absorb the varied talents of tens of thousands of mathematical men and women and keep them off the street. However, by Parkinson's Law, a million-dollar baby soon mushrooms into a billion-dollar monster, and these are figures which tend to chafe the sensitivities of taxpayers.

There are two ways to assuage the taxed: one is to stop the moon program and lower taxes; and a second one is to give the public something for their money. This NASA has done with aplomb.

The formula has been quite simple and successful. Pick one or two astronauts, make certain they have good-looking young families and shoot them into orbit in non-prime time. It is best to give the flight some purpose: flying in your underwear; flying without underwear; flying with a stewardess; and without one. The possibilities are endless.

At the beginning of each shot there is a certain amount of pad activity: a misfiring, trouble with the cigarette lighter, losing the key for the ignition, and the like. This builds tension and ratings. Then there is the inevitable countdown, blast-off, anxious views of the astronauts' wives going to church and to supermarkets and of the astronauts' children looking brave, and finally the climactic splashdown.

Now everybody on the IN knows that the astronauts do not actually *fly* the missiles. No one can live at that altitude or speed. But the recovery is so confusing and hectic that people tend to overlook that the two frogmen who rescue the rocket are really the astronauts in disguise. The triumphant arrival of the bearded heroes on the flight deck of a naval carrier obscures the details, and the Lindberg syndrome is once more successful.

It was the purpose of the NIMBUS flight to demonstrate the usefulness of inflight movies in space capsules, and so, armed with the reels of *Mary Poppins, Doctor Zhivago, Dear Brigitte, M,* and *The High and the Mighty,* the bullet rose quite majestically into the gray-blue Florida dawn.

But no one had informed NASA that one of the astronaut's wives had undergone rhinoplasty, commonly known as a nose job, and that her pert little face would be swathed in bandages for weeks. The space agency was at a standstill because no news media would possibly cover an astrorelative thus temporarily disfigured. The *Journal of Oto-Rhinology* might cover the subject briefly but no major media would touch it. No nose— no news. It's an old dictum in communication.

So there sat Chip Mate, the NASA Project Director, in the operations room watching Batman on the twenty-odd TV screens in front of him, endlessly munching matzos and yelling, "Keep 'em circling till that bandage comes off his wife."

"But what if the operation isn't a success?" an assistant meekly asked.

"Which one, NIMBUS or Nose?"

"The Nose."

"In that case we'll bring back two monkeys. Just get them into frogman suits at recovery."

"Two monkeys?"

"Yes. That should shake the Darwinists a little, don't you think? But get married monkeys with good-looking wives."

"Chip, Check. I mean, Check, Chip."

But NASA does not justify its folly merely by entertaining the public. It even goes so far as to create huge useless payrolls which are highly coveted by ocean-front communities. This economic opportunity was hardly lost on the Gutter brothers, who enlisted the help of Mayor Taft, and even the local A.G.A.I.N.S.T. chapter in trying to create a launching site in Ramona Beach.

"We've got everything Cape Kennedy's got," the Gutters reasoned. "An ocean and a shore."

"No one could argue with them, and soon every effort was made to woo Wernherr von Schmutz of NASA to study the merits of their case.

Von Schmutz was a legendary figure in space science. A strapping six-footer of German ancestry, he wore a square monocle and carried a high voltage swagger stick with which to instill efficiency in his subordinates. Working for Hitler in World War II, his efforts had almost brought England to her knees. Working for the Russians, his genius helped galvanize the Iron Curtain. When an even higher offer came from NASA, he accepted with alacrity and open hands. He was a true soldier of fortune, having made a fortune whenever his services were needed.

His interest in space dated from childhood. At the tender age of twelve he had blasted his parents into space, where they are probably still orbiting, by placing dynamite under their summer cottage during the Oktoberfest, a time of usual noisy merriment in dear old Munich. Once, on the Susskind show, he reminisced that he watched a rather sloppy lift-off, but his technique improved with the years, as he orbited endless "volunteers," even ex-wives, under varying and often trying circumstances. Whenever international tensions called for his talents, he was ready, a seasoned blaster, a giant of outer space.

Von Schmutz was a pleasant, quiet man; his associates at NASA Space Center referred to him affectionately as "the Swine." He had the world's foremost collection of shrunken heads, which were tastefully displayed about his orderly villa on Kraut Hill, and his name will certainly go down in history as the inventor of the countdown. A NASA archivist discovered some details of this from an aging mathematics teacher in Munich who claimed that when he tried in vain to get little Wernherr to count from one to ten, he finally yelled in desperation, "Start with ten and count down." But both men, the archivist and the mathematician, died under strange circumstances, and the facts will forever remain unclear.

Von Schmutz sat quietly in the lobby of the Ramona Biltmore, studying Chinese and waiting for his hosts Mayor Taft, the Gutter brothers, a delegation of ladies from A.G.A.I.N.S.T., all of whom, for various selfish reasons, hoped to persuade him to recommend a space center for Ramona.

Bearing beer and sausages and a superb shrunken pigmy head, they soon got von Schmutz on a first name basis and bandied the taxpayers' millions about like so much petty cash in the coffee-break box.

"We have the climate and the ocean," Taft stated.

"You will be closer to the enemy," the A.G.A.I.N.S.T. delegation argued.

"We've got the money," the Gutters said, "to make it worth your while."

Since all these sessions were secret, it will never be known exactly what, or how much, persuaded von Schmutz to designate Ramona as a NASA Launch Center, but a satisfied smile could be seen on the scientist's face as he goose-stepped along the strand in the early morning hours in the following weeks.

It was on one of these early excursions that von Schmutz quite by accident came upon Captain Sabella working on his balloon. Ever air-minded, he accosted the balloonist who was busily mending the straw in his basket.

"Wot is dis?" von Schmutz asked of Sabella.

"What do you mean, 'Wot is dis'?" Sabella said, looking up briefly from his labors.

"Dis gas bag."

"Dis gas bag is a balloon."

"Ja, ja, I know, but what is it for?"

"Balloons are for ascension," Sabella said patiently.

"Ascension to where?" von Schmutz asked.

"Into the *air*—the *air*," Sabella said, stabbing his fist skyward.

"I know the *air*, the *air*. I'm Wernherr von Schmutz."

"Wernherr von Schmutz? From NASA? The Swine?"

"*Please*. That is a nickname."

"Well, if you're who you say you are, why are you asking all these dumb questions? I've told you the balloon is for ascensions."

"I know, ascensions," von Schmutz repeated. "Useless, purposeless ascension."

"Can you tell me a better reason but to enjoy the wind, the view?"

"The only reason for the *air*," von Schmutz lectured, "is to allow man to drop things from an altitude."

"Like bombs?" Sabella asked.

"Precisely, bombs, missiles, rockets. The air is tactical."

"The air is polluted," Sabella said, "not tactical. It is very polluted right where you're standing. If you don't move on, I'll call the Air Pollution Squad."

"You are insulting me," von Schmutz said.

"We are finally in agreement. *Arrivedérci—Boche!*"

Lady Trilby had other worries besides her bearded boarder, Mayor Taft and the Afternoon Society. It was hardly fair, she thought, to accept the monthly stipend of a hundred pounds from the Crown and do nothing more for it but to complain endlessly about the ghastly conditions in the colonies. After all, had she not picked this post because of its challenge? Merely recognizing the problems was a long way from solving them, and detailing the foibles of the natives in her nightly report would only cram another musty filing cabinet for some future historian. What could anyone point to and say, *This* we owe to Lady Trilby? She felt she had to initiate some project, yes public works project—sewers, fortifications, rural electrification, a tube, of course. Ramona did not possess a tube. The poor natives would be totally helpless and exposed should the Nazis decide again to launch their bombers. With characteristic speed, she managed to get an appointment with the head of the Department of Public Works. He was a rather charming bald little man, who was quite famous for walking about the town with a carpenter's level which he placed on endless horizontal surfaces, watching the little bubble come to rest and then making notations in a loose-leaf binder which he carried in his hip pocket.

"You wouldn't realize it, Lady Trilby," he said, "but nothing in Ramona Beach is on the level."

"I would, Mr. Casparian, I would indeed."

He whipped out his little book and placed it almost under the nose of his visitor.

"I've been making studies for years. This town is crooked."

"Some of it, I heartily agree, some of it, but I've come to tell you of my plans."

"Go right ahead."

"What this town needs," Lady Trilby said, "is a tube."

"A what?"

"A tube."

"A tube of what?"

"How do you say it here?" Lady Trilby fidgeted with the head of her cane. "An underground."

"Oh, no!" Casparian jumped to his feet. "No underground. Don't you use words like this in a public office."

"I'm not making myself clear, obviously, Mr. Casparian. An underground railway."

"Oh a subway, you mean a subway?" Casparian was quite amused.

"I hope it's only my choice of words which is amusing you. I'm quite serious about the project."

"Where do you propose it to go? We're just a little town."

"It matters very little where it goes, Mr. Commissioner. If it hadn't been for the tubes, the citizens of dear old London would be annihilated today."

"You're not speaking of a subway at all then, you're speaking of an air raid shelter. We do have some Civil Defense money allotted to us, come to think of it. It's never been touched."

"Capital, capital." Lady Trilby rose and rubbed her hands as she paced the Commissioner's office. "I suggest we put the first stretch of road from Magnolia to First Street."

"Wait a minute, wait a minute! I said we had funds available for an air raid shelter, not a subway."

"Now you wait a minute, Mr. Casparian. I spent many nights in the Charing Cross station. Hundreds of us did, I remember, and I daresay morale would have been much lower if we didn't have the tracks that led into the tunnels. The trains didn't run during the bombings, but the tracks gave us hope. We knew someday we would triumph and a train would once again emerge from that hole all lit up and pretty with Bovril Bouillon ads splashed along its sides."

Casparian was not an insensitive man. He took out his level and placed it on the window sill. When the little bubble had come to rest in its glass container, he pointed to it. It stopped a few degrees to the left of center. "You see?" he said. "Crooked."

"A bit to the left."

"Yes," Casparian agreed. "Who's going to bomb us?"

"The Germans, I suppose."

"I thought they lost the war."

"Well," Lady Trilby said, rather softly, "you know I am the British Ambassador to Ramona Beach."

"So I've heard."

"In that capacity I am privy to certain information you may not be aware of. Now"—Lady Trilby brought out her own notebook—"how much Civilian Defense money do you have?"

Casparian scratched his ear. "I'm not sure. Maybe a million, maybe two. I'd have to check with Accounting."

"Well, that should be quite ample. Let's start with the first station, say on Magnolia Street. Build a proper stairway and a station underground. Lay some track into a short tunnel. You'd be surprised, in no time people will start getting into the habit of using the facility."

"Just build a station but no trains?"

"Yes," Lady Trilby said. "No civilized city is without a tube. You have no idea what it would do for the natives. Create employment, a proper shelter and civic pride."

There is, Casparian thought, a certain logic even to idiocy; he had been in politics long enough not to belittle any project which would create employment, shelter and civic pride. He also knew that Lady Trilby was backing the opposing mayorial candidate and was well aware his own position was an appointive one. What did *he* care how Civilian Defense money was to be spent? What did anyone care?

"Well, Lady Trilby, how do you propose to start?"

"I shall need some shovels. Good sturdy shovels with seasoned oak handles."

"I should have thought of that myself," the Commissioner allowed. "I shall have them delivered to the Embassy in the morning."

"Yes, some shovels, and perhaps a sign."

"A sign?"

"Yes. Magnolia Street Station. I think it would lend a real air of urbanity to Ramona."

"A sign," Casparian mused. "All right, a sign. I just would like to get one thing straight, Lady Trilby."

"Yes?"

"You're proposing a subway station which leads to nowhere."

"Let's just say, Commissioner, it is the world's first pure subway station."

"The first pure subway station?"

"Yes," Lady Trilby said, standing up rather abruptly and heading for the door.

"I'll send over the shovels in the morning."

"That will be fine."

"And the sign when it's painted."

"The sign, yes. You must excuse me."

Lady Trilby pushed her little golf cart to the very limit. At home she found the Stoltz brothers working in her back yard.

"How is the elevator coming?" she asked.

"Very good, very good." The Stoltzes nodded. "Would you like to take a ride? It's almost finished."

"No, no, I shouldn't want that." She looked at the structure towering above her. "Didn't you say this was the first pure elevator in history?"

"That's right." The Stoltzes nodded quite proudly.

"Well, if you can forgive an old fool, I should be quite proud if you'd dedicate that book to me."

She turned and walked to the flagpole and silently the two men watched her lower and fold the Union Jack.

21

. . . .

Although Thomas had decided to run a no-nonsense campaign and refrain from kissing babies, endorsing navel oranges or hanging sashes about bikinied low-fat buttermilk queens, he displayed true political showmanship in delivering his first speech from the top of the completed Stoltz steam elevator. It was a pretty structure, bedecked for this occasion with red, white and blue bunting. The antique bronze car gleamed in the fading rays of the afternoon sun. A huge sign on the third elevation proclaimed, "GO WITH WHITE, THE MAN ON TOP," and it took little urging to have the local citizenry assemble around the base of the structure to help Thomas launch his campaign.

Lady Trilby, beribboned and bemedaled, cut an imposing figure as she signaled the inauguration of the first pure elevator in history. Proudly Thomas stepped into the cab and rode to the top of the structure. He looked quite formidable, even to Pamela, who had to admit that whatever he lacked in family and eagle scouts he made up in youth and vigor, the necessary requirements for successful modern politics. His very first speech was simple and elegant. "You have a choice," he said, "between the quick and the dead. My opponent, backed by the Gutter brothers, wants to turn Ramona Beach into a sanatorium. Schools will be razed, homes will be condemned, the children deported. There'll be no music, no love, only decay and death. This vibrant sunburned town we love will be a staging area for the graveyard and the light of funeral pyres will rival the setting sun in the west. Gone will be the sounds of a close-meshed gearbox of a Jaguar, the bongos in the night, the electric guitars. All one will hear is a lonely horseshoe striking a pole on the beach, the organ music from countless funeral parlors, the sound of cards being shuffled for yet another game of hearts."

There was applause from the audience and Thomas

continued. "I look to the south and I see the ominous towers of NASA rising to spoil our lovely view and tranquillity. Another scheme of our Mayor and his cohorts. Soon we will live in the shadows of missile pads, the backwash of rocket propellants, the eerie sounds of jet engines fired in the middle of the night. Is this what we want for Ramona?"

The crowd roared, "No!"

"I do not propose we stand still. I am not against progress, full employment, the welfare of our citizens. I propose a subway for Ramona. A beautiful subway running from Magnolia to Beach Boulevard. It will give us a rapid transit system, a tourist attraction; it will create employment and shelter should we be attacked. I say, leave the heavens to the birds and the clouds; leave space to the stars; and leave Ramona Beach to Ramonans."

It was either the shock of hearing about the subway or the rhythmical progression of his speech which had captured the audience, but Thomas found his listeners hanging on every word.

"Now then," he concluded, "let me say that I will do my best to put local government into young and able hands, let me assure you that *my* only interests will be *your* interest, and may God give me strength to pursue my course."

Every politician likes to put God into his camp, but Thomas was also able to muster royalty to his cause—a gesture not lost on his audience.

"Ladies and gentlemen," he said, "I have the rare pleasure to introduce the honorable British Ambassador to Ramona Beach. She is a woman whose service to our community is too well known to need repetition, a woman whose courage saved us from the scourge of the Sweethearts, whose generosity kept many a surfer safe and sound. I give you, the Ambassador, Lady Isabella Thorbush Trilby."

The elevator descended gracefully to pick up the Ambassador and rose once more to its full height, bearing a proud and composed Lady Trilby.

"Ladies and gentlemen," she said, "I bid you hello on this great occasion. We are here to pay homage to two dedicated men, the brothers Stoltz, who built the first pure elevator known to man, and to inaugurate the campaign of my candidate, Thomas White."

The Ambassador paused and sipped a bit of Genoese wine.

"I've lived amongst you now for a number of months and I must admit you're a jolly good-natured lot. Warm, friendly, intimate to the point of embarrassment. You are pleasant to look at, and you hide very little. You are generous to a fault, neighborly, a bit noisy, but fortunately, I am blessed with a strong constitution and enjoy sleep no matter what is about. I've told Whitehall that you exhibit all the typical pleasant traits of natives of a subtropical culture."

Now Lady Trilby rose to full height.

"But enough of pleasantries. Let us not forget that you are beset with troubles. If you wish to stand on your own two feet, as a responsible nation in a world of responsible nations, you must change your entire attitude. To make *anything* out of this sunbaked wilderness will not only take a great deal of work and sweat from the young and able, but much guidance and wisdom from the older natives I see before me. Roll up your sleeves, put on your thinking caps. Get busy! To retire at your age to some mythical nepenthe, to think of leisure, lawn bowling, bingo, will not only spell disaster for the future of your country, but, let me assure you, the inactivity will prove harmful to yourself. Think over what I have told you. Study the issues at hand. Listen to the opposition. Weigh the purpose and the dedication of the candidates. And then? Then, do the proper thing. Cheers."

The reverberations of these valiant words soon made their way to Mayor Taft's office. The Mayor was not accustomed to having his office challenged; he was upset.

"How did they know about the retirement center?" he asked.

"We tried to hire White," the Gutters said. "He's a young architect. We thought he'd come cheap."

"This will complicate matters."

"I don't care how complicated things are," Gutter shouted, "we gotta win. Can't you call out the troops?"

"What for? There has to be a pretty serious local disturbance before I call on the National Guard."

"There's going to be," Gutter warned, "a pretty serious local disturbance if you lose."

"What do you want me to do?"

"Maybe you ought to go to Vietnam and visit the boys," Willi Gutter suggested.

"Why would the boys want to see me?"

"How should I know why they want to see you? It worked for Eisenhower. Take some cookies."

"It's not that kind of war," Taft said and dismissed the issue.

"What about the funeral directors' convention?" suggested Gutter.

"What about them? I told you they're coming the Fourth of July. A thousand strong. Embalmers, gravediggers, funeral directors, hearse drivers, organists, floral arrangers."

"I know they're coming. What have you got planned?"

"The usual thing. A band concert, parade, Iowa picnic."

"Nonsense," Gutter said. "These guys are big spenders. They like booze and broads. Why don't you have a beauty contest on the beach?"

"What do you want me to do? Pick Miss Stiff of sixty-seven?"

"That sounds better than an Iowa picnic. Funeral directors have a real sense of humor about their profession."

"I know," Taft said wearily. "I've been getting letters from their convention secretary. All their stationery is black."

"Well," Gutter said, "that's about the color of your future if you don't beat the kid."

"I know," Taft said. "I should have joined the Peace Corps like my brother. He's in Pakistan teaching the natives how to repair pinball machines."

"That's the Great Society for you," Gutter said, "real great for some. Not so great for others."

22

. . . .

Ramona Beach was no longer a peaceful beachside town a go go. Wernherr von Schmutz, the Mayor and his wily cohorts were pushing an ugly launching tower forty stories into the sky, a tower which would propel an ungainly bullet to rain unchecked terror on those below, while Casparian's Civil Defense construction men were busy planning a subway to protect themselves from just such folly. It all had the logic which justified automobiles because they make good ambulances, penicillin because it keeps alive gored bullfighters, and the thirty-five-hour work week because it supports the liquor industry.

To everyone's surprise, no project so thoroughly engaged the local citizenry as the Trilby Tube, the nickname given to the subway project. Even the Ambassador herself was amazed at the enterprise of natives when the women organized Teas for the Tube. The Elks Club had a Tube Stag and several of the churches threw Subway Socials. Soon the coffers were filled, and Lady Trilby found herself at the ground-breaking ceremonies on Magnolia Street.

There she was, amidst the bunting and the bands once more, facing a veritable army of workers, their shovels at the ready, like a battalion of Fusiliers poised for battle.

"Nothing," she said, "has warmed my heart so much as the sight of all of you ready for a proper day's work. And nothing," she added, "makes a man feel so good as a hole he has dug with his own shovel."

She nodded her head, the band played a chorus of "Rule Britannia" and Lady Trilby dug firmly into Magnolia Street with her trusty spade. There were cheers from all assembled, and she stepped into her golf cart to drive herself home, wondering where she had heard those stirring words. She decided it must have been at some socialist meetings she had attended in Soho when she was very young and pliable.

Within a few days the dedicated workers on Magnolia Street had reached a respectable depth of thirty feet. It was at this level that they made a startling archeological discovery.

At first it seemed they had merely run into a forgotten slab of concrete, but further digging disclosed the roof of an ancient building. The workers couldn't understand what had happened, but a retired local archeologist recognized the importance of their find and soon Ramona Beach was overrun by archeologists, prehistorians, and paleontologists who substituted delicate brushes, knives and forceps for the crude shovels of the workers.

This sudden scholarly activity proved quite amusing to all the people of Ramona Beach save Lady Trilby, whose exhortations to the workers to "keep digging" went unheeded. Captain Sabella agreed with her that nothing dug up from the past had ever helped anyone in the future, but even the dear Lady's ambassadorial powers were impotent in the face of the extraordinary discovery.

Nothing could dissuade the assembled scientists; evidence bore out that they had stumbled on the oldest human dwelling ever found; it predated the recent Nice discovery by at least 200,000 years. They were clearly dealing with a society unknown to archeological circles, for they had unearthed relics quite unlike the usual stone spoons and bowls, the fossilized remains of small animals, the ancient weapons.

Everyone connected with the project agreed that they had unearthed what could be called a prehistoric data processing center. Careful but feverish excavation revealed a room about forty feet square containing fossilized furniture, coffee machines, postage meters, beautifully preserved examples of lifetime guarantee ball-point pens, fossilized electric plugs and fossilized pin-up pictures on the walls. There were no human skeletons, but fossilized boxes of tissues and fossilized packs of filter cigarettes, even a sauna bath. But what fascinated the scientists most was a very large, very complicated pile of fossilized newspapers lying in the center of the room.

There it was, bearing an uncanny resemblance to the *Ramona Gleaner,* evidence of an early society as sophisticated as our own.

One short paleontologist whose interest had centered on the fossilized pin-up pictures soon confirmed the extraordinary sophistication this early society had enjoyed.

"My assistants and I have taken careful measurements

of the evidence," he announced to the press, "and allowing for rock shrinkage, geological compression, even a small clay deposit nearby, we are convinced beyond a shadow of a doubt that the ladies on these tablets are wearing mini-skirts."

Further proof was not needed. All men set about to unravel the mysteries of the newspapers.

Lady Trilby, dismayed at the work stoppage, met with little success in trying to revive the subway program, but she was a little more encouraged after speaking with the senior scientist of the project.

"You see," she pleaded, "I want to do something for the natives. This tube seemed such a worthwhile project."

"It was, Ambassador, it was, but you fail to realize the immensity of our discovery. You'll be famous all over the world."

"It is hardly fame I'm after," Lady Trilby said, a little hurt, "though I am not opposed to a statue."

"Neither am I," the scientist admitted. "I rather like the idea of standing between two diaphanous nymphs holding a test tube toward the horizon."

"I favor holding the flag," Lady Trilby said, "like this. Oh, I beg your pardon." She had abruptly raised her cane and knocked his glasses off.

"It's nothing," the poor man said, fumbling for his spectacles. "You see, the most intriguing part of this find is the old newspapers. If we could only decipher them, you have no idea the information it could give us."

It was not a futile wish, for the first breakthrough in the decipherment of the Trilby text (as it was finally called) came at 11:10 P.M. in a chilly hotel room of the Ramona Biltmore where the scientists had gathered. But their happiness was soon dimmed by the accounts they read. They clearly detailed an attempt by the ancient civilization to land a vehicle on the moon. The scientists could hardly believe the tragic fate which befell their forefathers when they attempted to explore outer space.

The newspapers carefully detailed the preflight activity in Ramona, the furious preparations (headed even in those days by an overbearing foreign scientist), and reported the last minute admonitions from sources on the moon for earthlings to cease their spatial activities. Later editions revealed that the crew, ever invincible, forged ahead despite repeated lunar warnings. The primitive countdown continued and blast-off occurred. The final story was quite short. The missile stayed on course and it traveled well over one half the distance to the moon. But at precisely 141,000 miles from earth it ran into a brick wall. The account ended poignantly with a late report that a tremendous earthquake was shaking Ramona Beach, a calamity that undoubtedly fulfilled the lunar threat to bury the earthlings who dared into space.

As the scientists finished the story, they looked outside their hotel window in dismay. To the south they could see the completed launching site of NASA, the men working furiously in the eerie fluorescent light readying the "bird" for blast-off. As devoted citizens of a moon-poised nation, the scientists could do no other but wire their findings to NASA headquarters, where the generals somewhat precipitously decided to cancel the moon program, seize the remainder of their billion-dollar appropriation and head for Las Vegas before civilization once more vanished from this planet.

It was a rather touching scene the next morning at NASA headquarters as Chip Mate stood in front of the thousands of employees in the parking lot.

"Fellow workers," he said speaking into a microphone. "I have ordered the Sixth Fleet to proceed to a point off the coast of Southern California to recover the NIMBUS shot. The mission was a complete success. Now, then, due to information received earlier this morning, I must tell you that this will end the space program." A great silence came over the audience. "You may pick up your final check from the accounting office, the Poverty Program will have mobile offices outside the gates and accept your application and the AVIS car people will give each of you a button reading 'We're number two but we try harder.' Good luck to you all and goodbye."

One sprightly old lady, a part-time semi-conductor sorter, asked weakly, "Why?"

"It's too far," Chip Mate said curtly and returned to the control center to guide his men into the Pacific.

Being good Americans, the NASA employees filed like sheep to the mobile Poverty Trailers that had been called in. All except Wernherr von Schmutz, that is, poised for blast-off in Ramona. Pacing in his beachside bunker, he ranted in German for several minutes and turned to the ever-present Gutter brothers and Mayor Taft.

"They are not going to abort my mission," he shouted. "They vill not abort. They vill not!"

"What do you mean they vill not; they have," said Willi Gutter.

"I have all the hardware I need, two monkeys, I mean astronauts, all the fuel, they can't stop me."

"You just can't launch a big missile without anybody noticing."

"Why not?" von Schmutz said. "Tomorrow is the Fourth of July. Who vill know the difference? One more explosion or less, the town vill never know."

"What about all the NASA guys working for you? They can read the papers, they'll know the space program has been canceled."

"I'll tell them we're just practicing, then at the last minute I blast. Ja. Blast, blast, blast!"

"Easy there," Mayor Taft said, putting a restraining hand on the frothing spacemaniac.

"I will change the trajectory just a little," von Schmutz said. "Just a few degrees up and maybe I'll get those monkeys to the moon."

"They're not monkeys," Taft said, "they're men. How you going to get them back?"

"My job is to get them there. Let *them* worry how to get back."

23

. . . .

By ten o'clock in the morning of the Fourth of July, the funeral directors' convention was already in high gear. Every available hotel, motel and wayside inn was filled with men dressed in black. Not to be outdone by the Elks, the Shriners or American Legion, they decorated their rooms with quaint little handmade signs, "Final Resting Place," "Home of the Stiff Ones," "The Casket Basket." Endless pitchers of martinis labeled "Embalming Fluid" were downed by members of the club with much gusto and devotion. And why shouldn't these men be happy? After all, a pleasant fun-filled day stretched before them. At one o'clock they could witness the annual grave-digging contest, at two o'clock there was the Hearse Race on Highway 99, at three o'clock there was an organ recital, at four o'clock there was a cocktail party hosted by the Safety Council, at five another party given by the National Rifle Association. There were fireworks promised for the evening, the Embalmers' Ball, a naval demonstration of Funerals at Sea, but mostly there was camaraderie, the casket salesmen, the florists, the headstone merchants, the embalmers, the men who consoled the bereaved, who read the lofty sermons, who polished the hearses, all joined in one common cause: money, happy to be in Ramona, happy to be alive.

After all, two thousand well-heeled merchants of death were bound to be welcome in a tourist-hungry little town, men who were eager to swap their black suits for Hawaiian print bermuda shorts and their professional look of somnolence to one of good clean alcoholic cheer.

Even Pamela White was somewhat shocked to see truckload after truckload of caskets which were to be displayed in the lobbies of the hotels where the conventioneers were staying. With awe and trepidation she listened to one salesman after another show his new spring line: mod caskets, caskets with built-in sunken bars, op caskets, pop caskets, urns in the shape of General MacArthur (complete with pipe, eternally aglow) or Thomas Edison (inventor of the eternal light), even a bowling ball with the deceased's last score engraved in gold.

But Pamela's interest in the funeral convention was really secondary, for she used the city's eagerness to publicize the event as a means of obtaining enough evidence to embarrass her husband's opponent. Using her shapely legs, her prestige as a reporter for a national magazine, and her unerring skill with a miniature camera, she ducked in and out of caskets, around floral displays, pipe organs, hearses, to dig out (as it were) the real story of the *real* merchants of death in Ramona. She precisely detailed all the shenanigans of Mayor Taft, the Gutter brothers, Wernherr von Schmutz and A.G.A.I.N.S.T. She outlined the schemes of these greedy men to level whole sections of Ramona, explained the presence of the funeral directors, the reasons for the NASA launching site, and documented those stories with pictures of the cashier's check made out to Wernherr von Schmutz, the architect's drawings for the proposed funeral homes, the Gutter earthmoving equipment poised on the hills outside of Ramona like an army of locusts ready for invasion. She had photographs of the shrunken head presented to von Schmutz, even pictures of his orbiting parents, and last, but not least, an admission from Mayor Taft's son that he was not an eagle scout at all, but only a Junior Birdman of America, a patriotic but much less exclusive society.

It is not easy to weigh *which* specific exposé most incensed the local citizenry, but any one of the accusations was sufficient to cause Mayor Taft to flee the city for Las Vegas, followed closely by the Gutter brothers, and the somewhat staggering funeral people, quite hurt that this inquisitive little girl had suddenly caused the locals to resent their harmless attempt at a little merriment.

24

· · · · · · · ·

By nightfall all of Ramona had read or heard of Pamela's exposure, and the citizens hastily decided to combine the annual fireworks demonstration on the beach with a victory celebration for their remaining candidate, Thomas White.

They gathered on that stretch of sand in front of the Embassy, erected a platform and summoned the municipal band. A huge bonfire was lit and fed by the hundreds of caskets left by the fleeing funeral people. Only the brilliance and color of the ascending fireworks rivaled the huge flames of the bonfire on the beach.

It is quite true that Pamela's investigations had rid Ramona of its enemies, but there were two men left who were unaware of her exposé: Wernherr von Schmutz and the Red Canary, the most dangerous spy of the Orient, who sat in the gathering darkness in his room at the Embassy surveying the goings-on below him with his spyglasses.

Not only was he confused by the conflagration below him and the unexplained explosives in the sky, but he had been quite upset by the influx of caskets into the community and the countless shiny hearses which he had barely managed to dodge with his Good Humor truck.

Unable to piece together all of the intricacies of the plot, he decided that it was time to act and rid Red China of all the figures he presumed dangerous to the motherland. He armed himself lightly (poisoned darts, a couple of hand grenades, a pet asp) and headed for the NASA launching site.

Wernherr von Schmutz sat in the bunkhouse near the new launching tower and stared at the red button which he would push in four hours minus thirty-eight. Forty stories above him, lying prone in their Gemini Eighteen capsule, the last two NASA astronauts innocently munched Milky Way candy bars, unaware of the dissolution of the organization, believing that the entire exercise was only a long practice maneuver, and debating various methods of lighting charcoal for a barbecue.

At precisely 7:31 von Schmutz ordered his two astronauts to take a final supper break. As they munched pizzaburgers in the underground NASA automatic cafeteria, von Schmutz climbed the ladder to reach the top of his space missile. There were 180 steps and the good imported lager beer slowed his progress, but he did finally manage to reach the command module of the spacecraft and seated himself in the pilot's seat to check out for the last time the proper workings of all systems.

Meanwhile, the Red Canary had managed to slip by the guards of the launching site. Even as von Schmutz crooned over dials and gauges, he sat in the bunkhouse debating which button would launch the missile towering above him. His well-trained spy sense made the task simple—for one of the buttons was still moist, obviously from the perspiration of the sweating German whose nervous forefinger had fondled its circumference for days. Dispassionately, the Red Canary pressed it and then watched as the two-hundred-foot spacecraft silently lifted off its launching pad and then screamed into eternity, where von Schmutz would undoubtedly rejoin his father and mother in some neighboring orbit.

Almost everyone in Ramona had gathered around the speaker's platform on the beach in front of the Embassy. All the good citizens, now rid of their evil Mayor, the threat of a retirement village, funeral parlors, even a NASA space center, stood happily around the rostrum watching the fireworks, listening to the patriotic strains of the gaily dressed municipal band, munching hot dogs, hamburgers, drinking pop, even some of the "embalming fluid" left by the routed conventioneers.

Thomas, with the true instincts of a politician, emerged from the Embassy, and his appearance galvanized the crowd into a cheering mob. He was chastely dressed in a blue suit, hatless, the very model of young American statesmanship, and only his sober words, his moving tribute to the efforts of his wife, made the citizenry quiet down and realize that the workings of democracy were indeed wondrous when a topless woman reporter could strip the veneer from a corrupt local government and a woman's love could gain for her man a prize which he so richly deserved.

"There are two women in my life," Thomas said, "and I owe my victory to both of them. One is my wife, Pamela, standing beside me, whose gallant exploits have exposed the wrongdoings of my opponents. The other woman is no stranger to Ramona. I am speaking of the honorable British Ambassador, Lady Trilby, who urged me originally to run for office."

Thomas bent down to massage his shin and then escorted Lady Trilby up onto the bandstand.

She was formally dressed in black, her red sash crossing her chest, her medals gleaming in the light of the bonfire. The good people cheered her wildly, but she finally quieted them down with a few good raps of her cane against the microphone.

She recognized many of the natives. There were the Stoltz brothers, those dear devoted men, Casparian, the tube diggers, the archeologists, and all the characters who had forever graced the beach in front of the Embassy. Sprinkled among them were some of the ladies of the Afternoon Society, even the surviving surfers and Sweethearts, their hair neatly combed, their faces smooth-shaven.

Finally she raised her eyes above them all and spoke.

"I stand before you tonight with mixed emotions. I should like to thank you one and all for being alive. Rest assured that any reference to you as brutal savages or subhuman inhabitants of a subtropical climate will prompt my most spirited defense in your behalf. Except for a few lost pounds, which I could well spare, I am in as robust health as the day I landed on your shores.

"Secondly," she said, "I share with you your enthusiasm for this fine young man you have chosen to lead you."

She turned to Thomas and pulled him alongside her at the microphone so all could hear their convocation.

"You, young man, have your work cut out for you. Do not glory in the power of your office. Try to finish the tube. Put some clothing on your people. Grow some decent food, till the soil, create some jobs. An honest day's pay for an honest day's work and leave the merriment for the Sabbath. I shall leave you the Service Manual. I've found it invaluable." She gave Thomas the Manual and faced the natives once more.

"I now come to the final point of my talk with you. Tonight I lowered the Union Jack for the last time in Ramona Beach. It shall no longer fly over the Embassy. It is officially closed as of this day. I do not want you to think, however, that I have made this decision lightly. I have not. For many years I've known of your impatience with the Empire and your desire for independence. I made it my duty to come here to guide you in this direction."

Drawing herself to her full height, Lady Trilby said, "Weighing all the pros and cons, watching you carefully all these months, listening to your arguments with the open mind of a civilized human being, it is my unhappy duty to tell you, with heavy heart, as the British Ambassador to Ramona Beach, as due and proper representative of Her Majesty the Queen, Elizabeth Regina, I do *not* grant you independence. But—and I say this not only as a cold emissary, but as a woman—I feel America shows great promise and I can assure you that when I give my official report to Whitehall in perhaps a fortnight—Captain Sabella's craft ascending and winds prevailing—I shall recommend another ambassador to land on these shores in fifty years to re-evaluate the situation."

She handed Thomas the Union Jack. "I present you the colors of our nation, young man, and I want you to fly it proudly."

"I shall always treasure it," Thomas said, kissing Lady Trilby on the cheek.

There was not a dry eye in Ramona, so hardly anyone noticed Captain Sabella's balloon next to the bandstand waving gently from its guy ropes. It was a pretty sight, the massive yellow and orange balloon with its wicker basket suspended only a foot off the ground. Captain Sabella stood by dressed in his best marine finery, his eyes shielded by an ancient pair of aviator goggles. He had affixed a Union Jack to one corner of the basket and the flags of Venice and the colors of Italy along the ropes which suspended it from the balloon. At the conclusion of Lady Trilby's speech he strode to his craft and with great agility swung over the side of the basket. He stirred the embers of his brazier and felt the slowly swelling balloon tug at its mooring lines. He checked all his equipment, and when he felt secure that everything was in readiness, he nodded to Lady Trilby to board the basket.

Lady Trilby acknowledged Captain Sabella's invitation and fished into her trusty knitting bag and retrieved an old-fashioned gold watch on a heavy chain. She opened the lid by flicking a lever near the stem and smiled at seeing a faded picture of her grandfather as a boy. He was really a rather grotesque human being. However, she could not dwell on those familial foibles, and observed the graceful hands on the face of the watch.

"Good heavens," she said. "It is eight-thirty already. I have a long journey ahead of me and all of *you* should be in bed if you hope to be at all productive tomorrow." Her audience was still quiet, stunned, Lady Trilby wanted so desperately to leave them with something monumental.

"If Captain Sabella's balloon ascends properly, I bid you farewell. If he has not mastered the art, bits and pieces of me will return to you in a trice. I beg of you, bestow them to the Pacific. I've become quite fond of your ocean. Cheers and God save the Queen."

Thomas and Pamela escorted her from the bandstand and she shook hands with the Stoltz brothers and all the natives who could manage to reach her. Then with a courtly gesture Captain Sabella ushered Lady Trilby into his wicker basket, already quite filled with all of her earthly possessions. She watched intently as the heat of the coals filled the prostrate bag to its ultimate oval fullness. Only at the last minute did Captain Sabella hand over his bottle of wine to one of the Stoltz brothers, standing fearfully on the beach with his fingers in his ears. But neither the Stoltz brothers nor the cheering waving natives had to fear anything this evening. When the last line was cast off, Captain Sabella and Lady Trilby rose beautifully and gently from the beach, past the bandstand, past the first floor of the Embassy, and the second, even the chimney, the Stoltz elevator tower, soaring upward, upward, into the balmy night sky.

As they passed the fifth and final level of the elevator, the Red Canary, who had run all the way from the NASA launching to the Embassy to try and foil the departure of Lady Trilby, desperately blew his poison darts at their balloon. But he was too late. The Stoltz brothers, realizing with horror that their ambassadorial comrade was threatened, pulled the master switch, trapping the Red Canary at the top of the only pure elevator in the world. There he was, helpless—a bird in a gilded cage.

Once more the natives cheered and Captain Sabella and Lady Trilby waved triumphantly. But soon distance and the night faded their figures, and the large balloon seemed to shrink in diameter the higher it ascended.

High above the beach, Lady Trilby turned to Captain Sabella. "It all looks so peaceful from here," she said looking down. "That poor troubled country."

"All you British can ever think of is service," Sabella

said. "Let yourself go, Isabella. Feel the freedom of the air, look at the stars and the moonlight on the ocean."

"I am looking at all this, Captain."

"Doesn't it do anything for you?"

"Yes. It makes me wish I had a little Italian blood in my veins."

"So do I." Captain Sabella moved a little closer, but Lady Trilby put up her hands.

"Now, Captain, I want one thing understood."

"Yes."

"I am most appreciative of your offer to take me to my homeland, but—"

"But what?"

"Well, we are a bit cramped in this wicker basket, I certainly hope this propinquity will not cause any breach in etiquette."

The Captain retreated to his side and shuffled the coals. "It is the way you look at it, Isabella. To *you* this is a wicker basket, to me it's a gondola. That is an Italian word."

Lady Trilby remained silent for a minute, and then said, "Yes, and a pretty one at that."

They drifted peacefully east, the quiet briefly broken by the two shots fired by the Destroyer Escort *Thistle* far below them, which was finally delivering the missing two salvos.